# Renewing the Judeo-Christian Wellsprings

# Renewing the Judeo-Christian Wellsprings

EDITED, WITH A PREFACE, BY
DR. VAL AMBROSE MCINNES, O.P.

A Tulane Judeo-Christian Studies Edition
CROSSROAD • NEW YORK

1987

The Crossroad Publishing Company
370 Lexington Avenue, New York, N. Y. 10017

Printed in the United States of America

Designer: Joanna V. Hill
Typeface: Galliard
Typesetter: G&S Typesetters, Inc.

LIBRARY OF CONGRESS CATALOGING IN PUBLICATION DATA

Renewing the Judeo-Christian wellsprings.

Includes bibliographies.
Contents: The George Hitching Terriberry memorial lecture: Jewish territorial doctrine and the Christian response / W. D. Davies—The Nina Booth Bricker memorial lecture: The idea of a people of God / John Macquarrie—The Rabbi Julian B. Feibelman memorial lecture: Toward a Jewish theology of Christianity / Jakob J. Petuchowski—[etc.]
  1. Judaism—Relations—Christianity.   2. Christianity and other religions—Judaism. I. McInnes, Val A.
BM 5 3 5.R447     1987        261.2'6        86-24909
ISBN 0-8245-0832-7

Frontispiece photograph of Ivan Mestrovic's sculpture of Christ and the Samaritan woman at the well from the New Orleans Vatican Pavilion is by Frank Methe.

To His Holiness, Pope John Paul II
To Rabbi Elio Toaff

To the students at Tulane University, who, by their interest, have helped to uncover the wellspring and who are renewing themselves academically in the living waters of God's revelation. May the seeds planted and watered by the Judeo-Christian tradition bear much fruit.

You must strike the rock,
and water will flow from it for the people to drink.

Exodus 17:6

Bring us something to drink!

Amos 4:1

The water that I shall give will turn into a spring inside him, welling up to eternal life.

John 4:13−14

# Contents

Preface    xi
DR. VAL AMBROSE MCINNES, O.P.

*The George Hitching Terriberry Memorial Lecture*

Jewish Territorial Doctrine and the Christian Response    1
W. D. DAVIES, DUKE UNIVERSITY DIVINITY SCHOOL

*The Nina Booth Bricker Memorial Lecture*

The Idea of a People of God    30
JOHN MACQUARRIE, CHRIST CHURCH COLLEGE, OXFORD UNIVERSITY

*The Rabbi Julian B. Feibelman Memorial Lecture*

Toward a Jewish Theology of Christianity    41
JAKOB J. PETUCHOWSKI, HEBREW UNION COLLEGE, CINCINNATI

*The Hugh McCloskey Evans, Jr., Memorial Lectures*

The Greek Bible: Hidden Treasure for Jews and Christians  53
ROGER LEDÉAUT, THE BIBLICUM, ROME
Jewish Tradition and New Testament Interpretation  72
ROGER LEDÉAUT, THE BIBLICUM, ROME

*The Nathaniel P. Philips, Sr., Memorial Lectures*

Sons of God and Ecclesia: An Intertestamental Analysis  89
HARALD RIESENFELD, UNIVERSITY OF UPPSALA, SWEDEN
The Hermeneutic Circle—Uses and Abuses in Translating the Bible  105
HARALD RIESENFELD, UNIVERSITY OF UPPSALA, SWEDEN

*The Nina Booth Bricker Memorial Lectures*

Jesus the Jew  122
GEZA VERMES, THE ORIENTAL INSTITUTE, OXFORD UNIVERSITY
Jesus and Christianity  136
GEZA VERMES, THE ORIENTAL INSTITUTE, OXFORD UNIVERSITY

# Preface

ON THE THIRTEENTH OF APRIL, 1986, Pope John Paul II made a historic visit to the main synagogue of Rome, where he was greeted by the Chief Rabbi of Rome, Elio Toaff. Their warm embrace, captured in a historic photograph, symbolizes a new climate in healing after almost two thousand years of misunderstanding and division between Christians and Jews. These two religious men sum up in their own persons the desire of Jews and Christians to be reconciled with each other in the one God. This sincere and unique embrace, therefore, sent new hope and joy throughout the world, reinforcing the common brotherhood we share as sons and daughters of the living God. The importance of such a dramatic gesture of friendship should not be underestimated.

The climate for renewal in the Jewish-Christian religions goes back to the Second Vatican Council when on October 28, 1965, the bishops of the Roman Catholic Church proclaimed the unity among all individuals and nations of peoples because of their common birthright as the children of God and heirs to his Kingdom. The Declaration *Nostra Aetate* provided the common ground on which to base a new dialogue with a view to better understanding between Christians and Jews. (Documents of Vatican II, ed. Flannery, 1975, 738−743).

Pope John XXIII, more than anyone else, gave a new impetus to the Judeo-Christian dialogue by calling the Second Vatican Council. In fact this new dialogue is the heritage that he has given to our age. Pope John Paul II has continued that new heritage, and thanks to the generous hospitality of the Chief Rabbi of Rome, that dialogue took on a new dimension when the Bishop of Rome took the unprecedented step of visiting the main synagogue of Rome.

After the Chief Rabbi graciously welcomed the Holy Father, the Pope expressed words of gratitude for the visit. He also spoke words of abhorrence for the genocide decreed against the Jewish people during the Second World War, which led to the holocaust of millions of innocent Jews. He recalled how, in those dark days of racial persecution, the doors of the religious houses and churches of Rome and of the Holy See were thrown open to offer refuge and safety to many Jews of Rome and throughout Italy.

At this historic meeting in Rome, Pope John Paul II emphasized that the decisive turning point in the relations between the Catholic Church and Judaism (and with individual Jews and Christians) was occasioned by *Nostra Aetate*. He went on to emphasize three points that are especially relevant for today's dialogue.

> First, the church of Christ discovers its "bond" with Judaism by "searching into her own mystery." The Jewish religion is, in a certain way, "intrinsic" to our own religion. We have a relationship with Judaism we do not have with any other religion. "You are our dearly beloved brothers . . . you are our elder brothers."
>
> Second, no ancestral or collective blame can be imputed to the Jews as a people for "what happened in Christ's passion." There is no theological justification for discriminatory measures or, worse still, persecution of the Jewish people. The Lord will judge each one "according to his own works," Jews and Christians alike.
>
> Third, notwithstanding the church's awareness of its own identity, it is not lawful to say that Jews are "repudiated or cursed," as if this were taught or could be deduced from the sacred scriptures. The Second Vatican Council also said this in the dogmatic constitution *Lumen Gentium* (No. 16), referring to St. Paul in the letter to the Romans (11:28–29), that the Jews are beloved of God, who has called them with an irrevocable calling. God does not repent of his gifts. (Doc. NCNS, 20 April 1986)

After the Pope's statement to the congregation of the Roman synagogue, the lingering phrase that caught the attention of all present (and
the media as well) was the reference to the Jewish people as "his elder
brothers" in the Faith. It is on this basis of common faith and common
brotherhood that the Chair of Judeo-Christian Studies at Tulane University was established. The historic genesis for the Chair mirrors in
a smaller way the larger historic developments of the Second Vatican
Council that have laid the foundation of a new age of interreligious dialogue between Christians and Jews.

At Tulane University in 1969, this new age of interreligious dialogue
developed concretely when students from our School of Medicine at
Tulane University expressed their concern about human values. They
felt that the intense scientific demands made upon them in the regular
curriculum ought to be balanced by a consideration of the moral and
ethical aspects that are inevitably encountered in the practice of medicine. These considerations prompted Dr. James Knight, then dean of ad-
missions of the medical school, to invite Dr. Sam Sanford and myself,
both chaplains with training in moral philosophy and theology, to discuss the possibility of an elective in that area. Such an elective in human
values was approved and implemented.

It quickly became evident that almost all of the students were woefully
deficient in religious knowledge and that their understanding of their
Jewish-Christian heritage needed clarification, reflection, and further
development. To remedy this basic problem without neglecting the prag-
matic demands of a clinical methodology, more time had to be made for
the study of foundations and sources. Thus the desire of medical students for the integration of their religious, ethical, and moral heritage
with their scientific training led to the serious consideration of how the
wellsprings of the Judeo-Christian tradition could best be made available to them.

Similar academic concerns began to be voiced on the uptown campus
of Tulane, where students began inquiries about a major in religious
studies. The philosophy departments at Tulane's Arts and Science College and at Newcomb College thereupon widened their offerings in that
area and inaugurated courses leading to a major in religious studies.
The chaplains at the university had for some time been aware of the

need for an in-depth treatment of the Jewish-Christian religious traditions. In addition to normal pastoral concerns, the religious centers on campus had indeed offered informal courses, but because of the lack of professional scholarship and method, no academic credit was granted for those courses.

With these facts in mind, the chaplains at Tulane University met in the spring of 1977 with the then-provost of the university, Dr. Robert Stevens, and with the vice-provost, Dr. Frank Birtel, to discuss the pastoral and academic role of religion. The university representatives expressed their warm appreciation for the positive steps taken by the religious centers to assist students in their struggle for spiritual and intellectual maturity. At the same time, they stressed the need for a stronger academic dimension to complement that which was already available at the university.

On the question of funding, a note of caution was urged, as money was difficult to raise. The chaplains confidently suggested that people might be inclined to support a University Chair of Judeo-Christian Studies in the hope that through it the intellectual quality of generations of students might be greatly improved. Following this suggestion, it was informally moved that I be appointed chairman to explore, both within the university and in the greater New Orleans communities, the possibility of funding the establishment of such a chair. Two committees were formed, one academic and the other financial, and working in close collaboration, they proposed the fall of 1979 as the most feasible time for setting up the chair.

The president of the university, Dr. Sheldon Hackney, and the board of administrators endorsed the idea and approved an informal drive for funds, confident that support for the idea would not be lacking. They had judged accurately, for within two years a million-dollar endowment for the chair had been raised. With financial support assured, I was then appointed executive secretary for the chair by President Hackney. When Professor Frank Birtel became provost of Tulane University, he headed the Committee for the Chair of Judeo-Christian Studies with vigor and enthusiasm and oversaw the appointments. Subsequently, Tulane's new president Eamon Kelly and Provost Francis Lawrence have wholeheartedly endorsed the academic work of the Chair. Students have enrolled in the various courses, developing their knowledge of religious studies.

Many of these students have gone on to graduate studies in some of the leading schools of religious studies.

These introductory remarks serve to explain how the Chair of Judeo-Christian Studies came to Tulane University. The chair will help students acquire a deeper understanding of their origins, traditions, and value systems, providing them with lectures by scholars highly qualified in religious studies. Tulane's chair is not unique, but it is a good illustration of how a tiny seed—the students' request—through collaboration of faculty, deans, university administrators, and members of the board and the wider New Orleans community, has grown into a beautiful tree. The essays which are presented in this volume are some of the first fruits to be harvested from this tree watered by the Judeo-Christian wellsprings.

The inaugural lectures for the Chair of Judeo-Christian Studies have been given by some of the most distinguished biblical scholars in the world. The inaugural lecture itself was presented by the internationally recognized biblical scholar Professor W. D. Davis. His lecture set the stage for the high quality and academic excellence that have characterized all of the public lectures. He focused on the central place of the Land in Judaism. Jewish consciousness and self-identity are inextricably bound up with the Land and the mystery of Israel. Further, he illumined the different strata and meanings in which the Land, the Temple, and Jerusalem have in Judaism. The centrality of the Land is further developed by Professor Davis by giving the Christian response to these Jewish realities and what they mean in the Christian context.

From the historicity of the Jewish territorial doctrine, Professor John Macquarrie of Christ Church College directed our attention to the theological significance of the idea of the People of God, showing both the biblical and theological implications for Jews, Christians, and in fact for all of humanity. The idea of "the People of God" provides the basic theological foundation for the unity and diversity of all mankind.

Professor Jakob Petuchowski pursued the difficult theological question of the need for a Jewish theology of Christianity and a Christian theology of Judaism, stressing the fact that Christian theology needs an articulated attitude toward Judaism from which Christianity receives its basic meaning and legitimization. Likewise, the creation of a Jewish theology of Christianity bespeaks the need for Jewish theologians to address how the loving Father of the Jews is, in fact, the loving Father of all humanity. In exploring these needs, Professor Petuchowski exposed the thought of Moses Maimonides and Franz Rosenzweig in regard to the doctrine of the two covenants.

Professor Roger LeDéaut of the Biblicum in Rome explored the fascinating implications of the Greek Bible as a hidden treasure for Jews and Christians. By showing the evolution of the translation and the dramatically adjusted interpretations of the text to different historical milieu, he convincingly proved how flexible the translators were and how open the inspired text was to a "reinterpretation" as in the Septuagint version. Carrying through on the different methods of interpretation of Scripture, Professor LeDéaut drew on the Targum to show how Scripture was not separate from tradition, but that it was transmitted with its interpretations. The knowledge of the Torah alone was insufficient. Thus the teaching of Scripture can be conveyed realistically only by means of interpretations, which themselves become part of the newly translated text and which reveal a personality all its own.

Professor Harald Riesenfield of the University of Uppsala, Sweden, threw new light on the evolutionary and eschatological concepts of the "Sons of God" and "Ecclesia" by an intertestimonial study and analysis. Also, his study on the various levels of translating the New Testament from Aramaic into Greek and thence into Latin, and finally into the various vernacular languages, has produced conflicts about many questions of interpretation. Consequently, a special field of research called *hermeneutics,* the process of interpreting and understanding the text in terms of its context, has grown up.

Finally, the concluding essays by Professor Geza Vermes, the renowned Dead Sea scholar, on *Jesus the Jew* and *Jesus and Christianity* reveal a new sense of the historical Jesus in the context of his Galilean home, the Jewish customs of his day, and his own life lived out as a Jew. Continuity and discontinuity of Christianity with Judaism is stressed in the context of who was the real Jesus and where he is today.

All of these essays, the first fruits of the Chair of Judeo-Christian Studies, stress the urgency and fruitfulness of exploring in contemporary scholarship the growth of the Jewish-Christian dialogue today.

JULY 1986                    DR. VAL AMBROSE MCINNES, O.P.

# Renewing the Judeo-Christian Wellsprings

# Jewish Territorial Doctrine
# and the Christian Response

W. D. DAVIES

I SHALL HERE ATTEMPT to assess the nature and place within Judaism of the doctrine which in various ways asserts there is a special relationship among the God of Israel, the People of Israel, and the Land of Israel. Is that relationship primary or secondary, dispensable or indispensable? Was the territorial doctrine of Judaism one which could be ignored as necessity dictated, simply accidental and peripheral, or an aspect of Judaism without which Judaism would cease to be itself?

At first encounter the question would seem to be easily open to strict historical investigation and an unequivocal answer. Sources for the understanding of Judaism are abundant: the practice of Jews as it bears upon Eretz Israel has been and is open to public and private scrutiny. One would have thought that the proposed question could long ago have been settled. In the course of Jewish history and especially in this century, however, certain unavoidable factors have impinged upon Judaism that have both clouded and clarified the issue and compelled caution.

## The Marked Theological Tradition

Let us begin with the doctrine itself. Despite the vicissitudes of Jewish history, the sacred documents on which religious Jews have rested—the

Tanak, the Mishnah, the Midrashim, and the Talmud—the liturgies which they have constantly celebrated, and the observances which they have kept across the centuries all point to the Land as an essential aspect of Judaism. The reader is referred to *The Gospel and the Land: Early Christianity and Jewish Territorial Doctrine* (Davies 1974) for a fuller treatment. Here we merely summarize the main points of the evidence in defence of the position indicated.

Two Hebrew terms have to be distinguished: *'adamah,* soil, land, earth; and *'eretz* which, while not always clearly distinguished from *'adamah,* bears also the meaning of a politically defined territory. It is with *'eretz* in this latter sense that we are concerned—that is, with the Land of Israel as territory. The boundaries of the promised land are never precisely defined. As in the Talmud, the term *Land* is used here to mean the promised land (*'eretz*) of Israel.

THE EVIDENCE OF THE CLASSICAL SOURCES OF JUDAISM
It would be impossible within the limits of this lecture to examine the different ways in which the importance of the doctrine of the Land emerges in the Tanak. It finds its fundamental expression in the Pentateuch, but is also abundantly reflected in the other documents of the Tanak. Two elements in the understanding of the Land are central. First, the Land is regarded as promised or, more accurately, as sworn by Yahweh to the people of Israel. The history of the tradition concerning Yahweh's promise, on which there is no widespread critical agreement, is complex. The most probable development seems to be from the recognition of a promise of a territorial patrimony to Abraham to that of a more extensive territory to the people of Israel, probably under the impact of Davidic imperial ambitions. Alongside the belief in the promise, the conviction prevailed that this promised land belonged especially to Yahweh. Not only did it necessarily belong to him, as did all lands which he had called into being, but it was his peculiar possession to give to his own people: the election of the people was bound up with his promise to give his own land to them (Davies 1974). Out of the combination, or fusion (G. Cohen 1961, 39), of the three elements involved in the promise—God, the People, and the Land—there emerged what has to be regarded as an essential belief of religious Jews of the first century and

later of the indissolubility or eternity of the connection between these three realities.

This belief comes to clearest expression in the rabbinic sources: the Mishnah, the Midrashim, and the Talmud. That fact is remarkable and significant because across many centuries the Sages, the authors and preservers of those sources, for good reasons had increasingly suspected any disturbing concentration on hopes for a return to the Land in any messianic context as a delusion and snare likely to distract their people from the essential task of living obedience to the Torah. As we shall later insist, they came to accept the need to acquiesce in the exiled life and to cooperate in foreign lands with foreign rulers. But paradoxically, they continued to shower their praises on the Land, emphatically expressing their concern for it and recognizing the ultimate indissolubility of Israel's connection with it. The initial stimulus for this concern has been especially connected with the destruction of the Land by the Romans in the war from 66 to 70 C.E. Conditions in Palestine after 70 C.E. were economically difficult. As a result there developed an increasing tendency for Jews to emigrate from Palestine to neighboring countries, especially Syria. The need to encourage Jews to remain in the Land, and not to depart from areas in it where they were permitted to live, was so urgent that the Pharisaic leaders adopted a policy of extolling the virtues of the Land and encouraging settlement in it (Davies 1964, 295f.; G. Cohen 1961, 45f.). But important as they were, economic factors were not the sole or even main reason for the emergence of the doctrine with which we are concerned. As we have indicated, the roots of the emphasis on the Land are deep in the Tanak. The Tannaitic and other sources build on the Scriptures even though they respond also to economic and political realities. They point to the significance of the Land in the most unambiguous way. There is a kind of umbilical cord between Israel and the Land (G. Cohen 1961, 45f.). It is no accident that one-third of the Mishnah, the Pharisaic legal code, is connected with the Land. Ninetenths of the first order of the Mishnah, *Zeraim* (Seeds), of the fifth order, *Kodashim* (Hallowed Things), and of the sixth order, *Tohoroth* (Cleannesses), deal with laws concerning the Land, and there is much of the same in the other parts of the Mishnah. This is no accident because the connection between Israel and the Land was not fortuitous, but part of the divine purpose or guidance, as was the Law itself. The choice of Israel and the Temple and of the Land was deliberate, the result of Yahweh's planning. The connection between Yahweh, Israel, the Land, Sinai, the Temple is primordial: it is grounded in a necessity of the divine purpose and is, therefore, inseverable (Lev. Rabbah 13:2). And it is no wonder that the rabbis heaped upon the Land terms of honor and endearment. For them the land of Israel is called simply *Hâ-âretz,* the Land; all countries outside it are *ḥutz lâ-âretz,* outside the Land. In T. B. Berakoth 5a we read: "It has been taught: R. Simeon b. Yohai says: The Holy One, blessed be He, gave Israel three precious gifts, and all of them were given only through sufferings. These are: The Torah, the Land of Israel, and the World to Come."

We have seen that behind the glorification of the Land stood passages in the Scriptures. But in addition to this, two factors could not but increasingly stamp the Land upon the consciousness of Israel. The first is that the Law itself, by which Jews lived, was so tied to the Land that it could not but recall the Land. As we have already stated, one-third of the Mishnah deals with the Land and all the agricultural laws in it, as those of the Scripture itself, deal with it. Consider Leviticus 19:23, 23:10, 23:22, 25:2 and Deuteronomy 26:1. These verses make it clear that the agricultural laws are to apply "in the land." Further, only in Palestine could there be cities of refuge, which were so important in the civil law (Num. 35:9f.; Deut. 4:41f., 19:1f.). True, there are laws not contingent upon the Land, and the distinction between these and their opposites was clearly recognized. But the reward for the observance of the laws was "life in the land," as is implied in Mishnah Kiddushin 1:9–10. The Law itself, therefore, might be regarded as an effective symbol of the Land: it served as a perpetual call to the Land.

The second factor was that because it was the Land to which the Law most applied, the Land gained in sanctity. In Mishnah Kiddushin 1:9–10—in the references to the Land, the walled cities of the Land, the wall of Jerusalem, the Temple Mount, the Rampart, the Court of Women, the Court of the Israelites—it is the connection with an enactment of the Law that determines the degree of its holiness. And for our purposes especially, it is the applicability of the Law to the Land in Mishnah Kiddushin 1:6 that assures its special holiness. The implication is that Jewish sanctity is only fully possible in the Land; outside the Land only strictly personal laws can be fulfilled, that is, the moral law, sexual law, sabbath law, circumcision, dietary laws, and so on. Of necessity, outside the Land territorial laws have to be neglected. The exiled life is, therefore, an emaciated life, even though, through suffering, it atones. A passage in T. B. Sotah 14a expresses this point of view in dealing with Moses' failure to enter the Land. Moses, outside the Land, is a suffering servant who atones.

In light of the above, it is not surprising that both the gift of prophecy—the gift of the Holy Spirit—and the gift of resurrection of the dead were connected by some with the Land. For example, Mekilta Pisḥa I reveals both the affirmation of Israel as the only land fit for prophecy and the dwelling of the Shekinah, and efforts made to deal with the difficulties such a position confronted, for example, the fact that Yahweh had appeared outisde the Land.

Again, in the view of some rabbis, the resurrection was to take place first in the Land, and the benefits of the Land in death are many (Gen. Rabbah 96 : 5). Some urged that those who died outside the Land would not rise: but even an alien (Canaanitish) slave girl who dwelt in the Land might expect to share in the resurrection (T. B. Ketuboth 111a). At the end of the second century Rabbi Meir, at his death, required that his remains should be cast into the sea off the Palestinian coast, lest he be buried in foreign soil. There is no space or necessity here to enlarge further. The desire to die in the Land, to possess its soil, to make pilgrimages to it—all these manifestations of attachment to the Land—history attests. Enough has been written to indicate that the primary documents of Judaism, the Tanak and Tannaitic Midrashim and the Talmud, are unequivocal in their recognition that the Land is essential to the true fulfillment of the life to which Israel was called.

## THE LITURGY AND THE OBSERVANCE

The liturgical practice of the synagogue points to the same witness. Throughout the centuries, beginning with the fall of Jerusalem in 70 C.E., the conscious cultivation of the memory of the Land, concentrated in Jerusalem and the Temple, has continued in Judaism. The rabbis at Jamnia, in demanding that the *Tefillah* or *Shemoneh Esreh* should be said three times a day, morning, afternoon, and evening (Mishnah Berakoth 4 : 1ff.), had in mind, among other things, the perpetual remembrance of Jerusalem and the Land. The *Shemoneh Esreh* for the morning and afternoon service corresponded to the morning and afternoon daily whole-offerings in the Temple. There was no time fixed for the evening *Shemoneh Esreh,* but on Sabbaths and festivals the *Shemoneh Esreh* was to be said four times (there being demanded an additional *Tefillah* corresponding to the "additional offering" presented on those days in the ancient Temple). Three times daily, then, the Jew was required to pray; among other things, he was required to repeat the fourteenth Benediction (dated by Dugmore in 168–165 B.C.), the sixteenth (possibly pre-Maccabean), and the eighteenth (40–70 C.E.). These read as follows:

> Be merciful, O Lord our God, in Thy great mercy, towards Israel Thy people, and towards Jerusalem Thy city, and towards Zion the abiding place of Thy glory, and towards Thy temple and Thy habitation, and towards the kingdom of the house of David, the righteous anointed one. Blessed art Thou, O Lord God of David, the builder of Jerusalem. (Benediction 14)

> Accept [us], O Lord our God, and dwell in Zion; and may Thy servants serve Thee in Jerusalem. Blessed art Thou, O Lord, whom in reverent fear we serve [or, worship]. (Benediction 16)

> Bestow Thy peace upon Israel Thy people and upon Thy city and upon Thine inheritance, and bless us, all of us together. Blessed art Thou, O Lord, who makest peace. (Benediction 18)

That there was a deliberate concern with Jerusalem appears from the text in Mishnah Berakoth 4:1ff., where the rules concerning the *Shemoneh Esreh,* indicated above, are set forth, and where Mishnah Berakoth 4:5 states that, according to R. Joshua (C.E. 80–120): "If [a man] was riding on an ass [when the time for the prayer is upon him] he should dismount [to say the Tefillah: Danby]. If he cannot dismount he should turn his face [toward Jerusalem]; and if he cannot turn his face, he should direct his heart toward the Holy of Holies." The centrality of the Land is clear. The same is also emphasized in Numbers Rabbah 23:7 on Numbers 34:2. The deliberate recalling of the Temple and thereby of Jerusalem and the Land in the liturgy also appears from Mishnah Rosh-ha-Shanah 4:1–3 and T. B. Baba Bathra 60b.

Again other elements in the Jewish liturgy came to be *zêker l<sup>e</sup>hor<sup>e</sup>bân*, that is, in memory of the destruction. For three weeks of sorrow, ending on the ninth day of the month of Ab, which is given over entirely for twenty-four hours to fasting, Jews annually recall the destruction of their land. So much has that event become the quintessence of the suffering of Jewry that the ninth of Ab is recognized as a day on which disasters recurred again and again to the Jewish people. Connected with it significantly was the decree that the fathers should not enter the promised land. The passage in T. B. Ta'anith 29a that states this cannot easily be dated. But it is traced to an unknown rabbi whose words are explained by R. Hama b. Hananiah (279–320 C.E.). The pertinent passage is in Mishnah Ta'anith 4:6–7. As a matter of history, only the fall of Betar (the Beth Tor of the text), the last stronghold of Bar Kokba, captured by the Romans in 135 C.E., possibly occurred on the ninth of Ab. The first Temple was burnt on the seventh of Ab (2 Kings 25:8–9) or on the tenth of that month (Jer. 52:12); the Second Temple fell on the tenth (see the dictionaries). The essential feature of the liturgy for the ninth of Ab (which is the only twenty-four hour fast apart from the Day of Atonement) was the reading of Lamentations and dirges. Later, on the fast of the ninth of Ab, an addition that concentrates on Jerusalem still further was made to the service. The prayer, as used today, begins with the words, "O Lord God, comfort the mourners of Zion; Comfort those who grieve for Jerusalem." It ends with, "Praised are You, who comforts Zion, Praised are You, who rebuilds Jerusalem."

So far, in showing how the sentiment for the Land remained powerfully active in Judaism after 70 C.E., we have mostly adduced materials from the Haggada and the liturgy of Rabbinic Judaism. There was also a more specifically halakic approach to the question of the Land. The ramifications of this development we are unfortunately not competent to trace. We can only refer to two items. In the Jerusalem Talmud, in Kilayyim VII:5, ed. Krotoshin (or Venice) 31a, line 32 (Venice, line 25), Orla 1:2, ed. Krotoshin 61a, line 11 (Venice, line 9), there is a Jewish law which is quoted as giving to Israel a legal right to the Land. The law is translated by Lieberman as, "Though soil cannot be stolen, a man can forfeit his right to this soil by giving up hope of ever regaining it." The argument is that Israel never for a moment gave up hope of regaining the soil of Palestine. Never did they renounce their right to Palestine and never have they ceased claiming it in their prayers and in their teachings. It is on this foundation that [Jews] now claim that Eretz Israel belongs to them" (Lieberman 1949). Not unrelated to this law is that of $h^a z\bar{a}k\bar{a}h$ (prescription) in which the legal right of Israel to the Land was sought. (See *Baba Bathra* 28a, and notes in the Soncino translation for $h^a z\bar{a}k\bar{a}h$). But how early such attempts were and how significant in the discussion of the relationship between Israel and Eretz Israel in the period of our concern we cannot determine. The history of the halakic understanding of that relationship lies beyond the scope of this study, as does the relative place of Haggada and Halakah in Judaism. (J. Neusner [1979, 83–84] urges that "Halakah is Judaism's primary expression of Theology." Heschel would qualify this.)

Nevertheless, it is in the Haggada and the liturgy that the full force of the sentiment for the Land is to be felt. It cannot properly be seen except through Jewish eyes, nor felt except through Jewish words, such as those so powerfully uttered by Abraham Heschel in *Israel: An Echo of Eternity* (New York, 1969), which is more a lyrical outburst than a critical study, and in A. Néher's moving essay, "Israël, terre mystique de l'Absolu," in *L'Existence Juive* (Paris, 1962).

So far we have referred to the evidence of the classical sources of Judaism (G. Cohen 1961, 41). The same theological conviction that there is an inseverable connection between Israel, the Land, and its God continued to be cherished throughout the medieval period and up to the modern. A rough division has been drawn between two periods. The first stretches up to the last revolt of Jews in the Roman Empire in the hope of reestablishing a Jewish state which followed upon the imposition of harsh anti-Jewish statutes under Justinian (483–565 C.E.), and later the brief three-year reign of Nehemiah, a messianic figure, in Jerusalem from 614 to 617 C.E. It is legitimate to recognize up to that time a living, if intermittent, hope and violent activity directed toward the actual return of the Land politically to Israel. From then on, especially after the Arab conquest of the Land in 638 and the building of the Mosque of Omar on the site of the Temple in 687–691, a mosque that was to be a center for the Islamic faith, there was, it has been suggested, a change. Jewish devotion to the Land came to express itself for a long period not so much in political activity for the reestablishment of the state of Israel as in voluntary individual pilgrimages and immigrations to the Land (Marquardt 1975, 28n1). But the division suggested between the two periods must not be made inflexible. On one hand, in the earlier period the Tannaitic and Amoraic sages were wary of political attempts to reestablish the kingdom of Israel in its own land. On the other hand, in the Middle Ages there was much apocalyptic-messianic speculation and probably much activity aimed at such a reestablishment: the history of this has been largely lost, so that its full strength must remain conjectural even if likely. The extent to which apocalyptic-messianism persisted, to break out finally in Sabbatianism in the seventeenth century, is only now being recognized through the influence of the work of Gershom Scholem (Scholem 1973; Davies 1976). It fed into the Zionist movement of our times. What we can be certain of is that Eretz Israel, as an object of devotion and intense and religious concern, continued to exercise the imagination of Jews after the fall of Jerusalem in 70 C.E. and after the Arab conquest. It remained part of the communal consciousness of Jews. In this connection, two facts need to be borne in mind. First, the devotion to the Land is not to be simply equated with the imaginative notions of other peoples about an ideal land—such as the Elysium of Homer, the Afallon of Celtic mythology, the Innisfree of Yeats. Rather it was concentrated on an actual land with a well-known history, a land known to be barren and rugged and to offer no easy life though it was transfused because of its chosenness to be Yahweh's own and Israel's as an inheritance from him. Second, the influence of the familiar or customary division of history at the advent of Christ into two periods "before Christ" and *anno Domini,* has often tended to create the unconscious assumption among Gentiles that after the first century Jews *as a people* ceased to have a common history (Marquardt 1975, 107ff.). No less a scholar than Martin Noth saw Israel's history as having come to a ghastly end with the Bar Kokba revolt (Noth 1958, 448, 453f.; Klein 1975, 15–38). But the Jews continued as a people, not simply as a conglomerate of individuals, after that tragic event. The Talmud, the primary document of Judaism in the Middle Ages and afterward to the present time, concerns itself with the way in which the people of Israel should walk. The Talmud has a communal national reference in its application of the Torah to the actualities of the Jews' existence. Its contents, formation, and preservation presuppose the continuance of the self-conscious unity of the people of Israel. It is this that explains the character of the Talmud: it adds Gemara to Mishnah, and Rashi (1040–1105 C.E.) to both, to make the tradition of the past relevant to the present. It is realistically involved with the life of the Jewish people over a thousand years of its history (Marquardt 1975, 107f.).

And in the devotional life of the Jewish community, the relationship to the Land remained central (Werblowsky 1967, 374–75). To trace the various expressions of devotion to the Land among Jews across the centuries is beyond our competence. The most noteworthy is that of pilgrimage. The Law demanded that every male Israelite should make a pilgrimage to Jerusalem three times a year: at Passover, the Feast of Weeks, the Feast of Tabernacles (Exod. 23:17; Deut. 16:16). During the Second-Temple period even Jews of the Diaspora sought to observe this demand. (See, for example, Mishnah Taanit 1:3; Jos., *Wars* 6:9; Aboth 5:4.) After the destruction of the Temple, pilgrimages, especially to the Wailing Wall, became occasions for mourning: there were pilgrimages throughout the Middle Ages to other holy places. Individual Jews witness to this, a most famous example coming in the works of the "God-intoxicated" or "God-kissed" Jehudah Halevi, a Spanish physician born in Toledo in 1086. At the age of fifty, he left his beloved Spain on a perilous pilgrimage to Zion. He died possibly before reaching Jerusalem, but not before expressing his love for the Land and Zion in unforgettable terms. "My heart is in the east, and I in the uttermost west— How can I find savour in food? How shall it be sweet to me? How shall I render my vows and my bonds, while yet Zion lieth beneath the fetter of Edom, and I in Arab chains? A light thing would it seem to me to leave all the good things of Spain—Seeing how precious in mine eyes it is to behold the dust of the desolate sanctuary" (Brody 1946, 2).

It was not only single, individual pilgrims who sought the Land but groups of communities, as in the case of Rabbi Meir of Rothenburg who in 1286 C.E. sought to lead a great number of Jews from the area of the Rhine to Israel. Later, in 1523, David Reuveni led a messianic movement aimed at a return to the Land which attracted the interest of communities in Egypt, Spain, and Germany. The living Jewish concern to establish an earthly kingdom in Jerusalem may have contributed to the formulation of the seventeenth article of the Confession of Augsburg of 1530 (Marquardt 1975, 131). The justification for such a concern was made luminously clear in the astounding response to the Sabbatian movement from the Yemen to Western Europe (Scholem 1973).

These data to which historians point us cannot be ignored. However, we are not competent to assess the relative weight which should be given to the purely religious interest in the Land which led individuals and groups to journey to Israel out of a desire to experience the mystical or spiritual power of the Land rather than to a desire to escape and to right the wrongs of exile. Certainly many pious Jews had no directly political concern: their sole aim was to recognize that in the Land, as nowhere else, a relationship to the eternal was possible. A striking illustration of spiritual concentration on the Land is provided by Rabbi Nahman of Bratzlov (1772–80), who journeyed to Israel. He asserted that what he had known before that journey was insignificant. *Before*, there had been confusion; *after*, "he held the Law whole." But all he had desired was direct contact with the Land. This he achieved by simply stepping ashore at Haifa. He desired to return immediately. (Under pressure he stayed and visited Tiberias, but never even went up to Jerusalem.) Again, the celebrated Maharal of Prague (Rabbi Yehuda Liwa of Loew—Ben Bezalel, 1515–1609) understood the nature and role of nations to be ordained by God as part of the natural order. Nations were intended to cohere rather than to be scattered. Nevertheless, he did not urge a political reestablishment of a state of Israel in the Land; he left that to God. Exile no less than restoration was in His will; the latter *would* come in His good time, but only then. (The promise of the Land would endure eternally. Return was ultimately assured [Lev. 26:44–45]).

Due to the kind of devotion we have indicated, despite geographical and political obstacles, at no time since the first century has the Land of Israel been wholly without a Jewish presence, however diminished. The numbers of Jews living in the Land throughout the centuries have been variously estimated, but James Parkes rightly insisted that Jews in Palestine across the centuries were forgotten by historians. It is certain that in the nineteenth century, first under the influence of Rabbi Elijah, Ben Solomon Salman of Vilna, known as the Vilna Gaon (1720–1797), a number of parties of Jews, soon to be joined by many others, went to Safed in 1808 and 1809. These sought not simply contact with the Land of which they claimed that "even in its ruins none can compare with it," but permanent settlement (Vital 1975, 7; Marquardt 1975, 131ff.). Regarding themselves as representatives of all Jews, they assumed the right to appeal to other Jews for aid and reinforcement. Some, such as Rabbi Akiba Schlessinger of Preissburg (1832–1922), were driven to the Land by the realization of the increasing impossibility of living according to the Torah in Western society, which was becoming increasingly secular. For such people the Land became an escape and a refuge from modernism and secularism, a bulwark for the preservation of the religious tradition. After these early settlements to which we have referred, there were other efforts to reenter the Land by religious Jews whose history cannot be traced here. We must simply note that the Zionist movement, despite its strongly nationalistic, socialistic, and political character, is not to be divorced from this devotion to the Land. We shall deal with this later.

## An Inescapable Historical Diversity

I have sought in the preceding pages to do justice to the theological role of territory in Judaism. Jewish theology as revealed in its sources seems to point to the Land as the essence of Judaism. In strictly theological terms, the Jewish faith could be defined as "a fortunate blend" of a people, a land, and their God. But this view has been criticized because in any blend an item may be lost, and in the particular blend referred to, the essential and distinctive significance of the Land could be lost. As in discussions of the Trinity in which the personal identity of each member is carefully preserved and not simply blended, so in our understanding of Judaism the distinct or separable significance of the Land must be fully recognized. Judaism held to an election of a people and of its election to a particular land; Werblowsky (1967, 377) rightly speaks of "une vocation, spirituelle à la géographie."

But like Christian theology, Jewish theology has had to find ways of coming to terms with history. In this section we shall indicate certain actualities of Jewish history that must bear upon any answer to the question of the place of the Land in Judaism.

In the first place, historically the term *Judaism* itself cannot be understood as representing a monolithic faith in which there has been a simplistic uniformity of doctrine either demanded or imposed or recognized about the Land, as about other elements of belief. Certainly this was so at all periods and in all sections of the Jewish community before

70 C.E. And despite the overwhelming dominance of the rabbinic form of Judaism, the history of the Jews since that date, though not to the same degree, reveals the same fissiparous, amorphous, and unsystematized doctrinal character. The concept of an adamant, unifrom, orthodox Judaism, which was not stirred by dissident movements and ideas, and by mystical, messianic yearnings which expressed themselves outside of or in opposition to the main, strictly rabbinic tradition, is no longer tenable. To define the place of Eretz Israel in Judaism requires the frank recognition that that place has changed or, more accurately, has received different emphases among various groups and at different times. However persistent some views of and attachment to the Land have been, and however uniform the testimony of the classical sources, there has not been one unchangeable, essential doctrine universally and uniformly recognized by the whole of Judaism. There is an illuminating controversy that circled around Maimonides (Rambam [1135–1204]) during the Middle Ages. In his *Dalalat al Harin*, translated into English as the *Guide to the Perplexed*, the Great Eagle never concerned himself directly with "the Land." Although he was so concerned in his commentary on the Mishnah, his silence about the Land in the *Guide* caused dismay and dispute among the rabbis. Naḥmanides (1194–1270) was led to criticize the Great Eagle by insisting that there was a specific commandment (*mitzwah*) to settle in the Land, a mitzwah that Maimonides had ignored. Naḥmanides notes its absence in Maimonides' *Sepher-Ha-Mitzwah*. (For more information on Naḥmanides, see the *Encyclopedia of the Jewish Religion*.) In modern times Reform Judaism in the United States, anxious to come to terms with Western culture, was careful to avoid any emphasis on any particularistic elements in Judaism that would set Jews apart from their Christian neighbors. Until recently, when external and internal pressures made themselves felt, the doctrine of the Land tended to be ignored or spiritualized. It was an embarrassment.

The demotion of the Land, along with the messianic idea and its disturbing potentialities, was no less evident in the liberal Judaism of nineteenth-century Europe. Hermann Cohen reveals how far the confused and confusing embarrassment with the Land went there, even among Jewish theologians. In 1880 he claimed that Judaism was already in the process of forming a "cultural, historical union with Protestantism" (Vital 1975, 207n19). It is not surprising that he could write such paradoxical words as the following. *"The loss of the national state is already conditioned by messianism. But this is the basis of the tragedy of Jewish peoplehood in all its historic depth.* How can a people exist and fulfill its messianic task if it is deprived of the common human protection afforded by a state to its people? And yet, just this is the situation of the Jewish people, *and thus it must needs be the meaning of the history* of the Jews, if indeed this meaning lies in messianism" (H. Cohen 1972, 311–12; italics added). Cohen was concerned with the state and with Judaism, but by implication he not only questioned the messianic destiny of Israel in its own land, but, even if he still recognized it as a reality, he so domesticated that destiny in his Western Europe that it bore little resemblance to the dynamism of the messianism expressed in previous Jewish history. Cohen's messianism eradicated the Davidic Messiah and the hope of a kingdom of God on earth—and with this any hope for the Land. Even though the reform and liberal Judaism factions in the United States and Europe have recently reintroduced an emphasis on the Land in response to contemporary events which they could not ignore, that emphasis cannot obliterate their earlier nonterritorial or antiterritorial attitude. Not unrelated to this discussion in the reform and liberal Judaism, though not directly connected with those movements, is the insistence by such figures as Aḥad Ha'Am (1856–1927) that Jews first needed to devote themselves to spiritual renewal, not to the occupation of a territory. Aḥad Ha'Am founded a select and secret society in 1899 "dedicated to the notion that moral and cultural preparation had to precede the material salvation of the Jews" (Vital 1975, 156, 188–201).

Second, in a historical examination it is necessary to recognize that the territorial theology with which we are concerned could not but gain increasing attention and therefore emphasis among recent students of Judaism because of the pervasive influence of the Zionist movement. The ascribing of a theological concern with the Land to Jews who entertain no definable Jewish theology or who may even reject the tradition of their fathers has become insidiously easy because of the Zionist climate within which so much of modern Jewry lives. The temptation to this ascription has been reinforced by an understandable sympathy toward the justification of the doctrine that the suffering of Jews in modern Europe so imperatively calls forth.

But sympathy by itself does not necessarily lead to historical truth. At this point it is important to emphasize the complexity and interpenetration of the many forces that combined to initiate the Zionist movment. It held together apparently irreconcilable points of view in a living tension. Any neat dichotomies between religious and political factors in Zionism are falsifications of their rich and mutually accommodating diversity. To read Gershom Scholem's autobiographical pages is to be made aware of the impossibility of presenting clean, clear lines in any picture of the Zionist movement (*Jews and Judaism in Crisis,* 1–48). But this much is certain: the territorial theology of Judaism should not be ascribed directly (the qualifying adverb is important) to the many nonreligious Jews who played a most significant part in Zionist history. The Zionist movement, which has played so prominent a role in our time, was initiated by the Congress of Basel in 1897. It grew thereafter until in 1948, after an abeyance of almost twenty centuries, there emerged the state of Israel. But the role of Jewish territorial doctrine and sentiment in the movement has to be carefully assessed: it can easily be exaggerated. At first it was possible for some of the leading Zionists to contemplate the establishment of a state outside the Land altogether—in Uganda, in Argentina, in newly conquered Russian territories in Asia, in Asiatic Turkey, and in North America. The often silent but almost ubiquitous presence of the religious tradition, with its concentration on Eretz Israel, however, caused those leaders to change their minds and made the final choice of the Jewish homeland inevitable. Herzl, like other Zionist secularists, was compelled to recognize this.

But Zionism remained an expression not only, and probably not even chiefly, of the theological territorial attachment of Judaism, but even more an expression of the nationalist and socialistic spirit of the nineteenth century. In this sense it is a typical product of that century. An examination of the history of Zionism makes its specifically religious motivation less significant than an uncritical emphasis on territorial theology would suggest. Gershom Scholem, in reply to an article by novelist Yeuda Bourla, wrote:

> I . . . am opposed, like thousands of other Zionists . . . to mixing up religious and political concepts. *I categorically deny that Zionism is a messianic movement and that it is entitled to use religious terminology to advance its political aims.*

> The redemption of the Jewish people, which as a Zionist I desire, is in no way identical with the religious redemption I hope for the future. I am not prepared as a Zionist to satisfy political demands or yearnings that exist in a strictly nonpolitical, religious sphere, in the sphere of End-of-Days apocalyptics. The Zionist ideal is one thing and the messianic ideal is another, and the two do not touch except in pompous phraseology of mass rallies, which often infuse into our youth a spirit of new Sabbatianism that must inevitably fail. The Zionist movement is congenitally alien to the Sabbatian movement, and the attempts to infuse Sabbatian spirit into it has already caused it a great deal of harm. [*Ibid.*, 44]

It seems that Scholem would here largely recognize Zionism as comparable with other nationalistic movements such as those of Italy and many other countries in the nineteenth century. In a summary of forces which led to the triumph of Zionism, Scholem writes with greater fullness.

> If Zionism triumphed—at least on the level of historical decisions in the history of the Jews—it owes its victory preeminently to three factors that left their imprint on its character: it was, all in all, a movement of the young, in which strong romantic elements inevitably played a considerable role; it was a movement of social protest, which drew its inspiration as much from the primordial and still vital call of the prophets of Israel as from the slogans of European socialism; and it was prepared to identify itself with the fate of the Jews in all—and I mean all—aspects of that fate, the religious and worldly ones in equal measure. [*Ibid.*, 44]

In this admirably balanced assessment (which is as significant for what it does not contain, that is, apocalyptic territorial messianism, as for what it does) Scholem, while recognizing the role of the religious tradition, does not make it the dominant factor. To him Zionism was essentially a sociopolitical protest (Scholem 1973, 247). And in the judgment of many Jews, the Congress of Basel was important not primarily because it gave expression to a strictly religious hope for the Land, living and creative as that was, but because it also voiced a concern for the actual economic, political, and social distress and often despair of Jews in Europe; it was a response not so much to a crisis in Judaism and to an endemic territorial theology as to the plight of the Jewish people (Vital 1975, 375). To underestimate the secular character of much of Zionism and to overemphasize its undeniable religious dimensions is to lay oneself open to the temptation of giving to the doctrine of the Land a significance in much of Judaism that would be a distortion.

In the third place, the witness of history, at first sight at least, might suggest that Eretz Israel has not been the essence of Judaism to the extent that the literary sources and liturgies and observances of pious Jews and even the political activity of nonreligious Jews would suggest. Certain aspects of that history are pertinent. We have elsewhere indicated that there was a lack of any explicit appeal to the doctrine of the Land in the outbreak of the Maccabean revolt or the revolt against Rome in 66 C.E. This fact is striking (Davies 1974, 90–104). Even more overlooked have been the expressions in the Maccabean period of protests against and opposition to the Hasmonaean rulers who had created an independent state. (See Isa. 44:28; Ezra 1:1f., The Chronicler; Jos. *Antiquities* XII:3.3, 138f.; *Antiquities* XIII:13.5, 372f.; *Antiquities* XVII:11.1, 299f.; Diodorus, *Bibliotheca Historica* XL:2. Cf. Stern 1974, 185–86.) These protests made the later attitudes of the Pharisaic leaders in coming to terms with Roman rule and in declaring the laws of the Land, wherever Jews dwelt, to be Law, less innovative than has customarily been recognized (Scholem 1973, 31f.). And at this point, the nature of the rabbinic attitude across the centuries must be fully recognized. That the doctrine of the Land remained honored among the rabbis cannot be doubted. But despite the facts referred to in the preceding pages, after 70 C.E. until recent times, it was a doctrine more honored in word than in deed. After 70 C.E. the powerlessness of Jews against the Roman authorities left the rabbinic leaders no choice other than submission and acquiescence to their divorce from the Land. This submission and acquiescence were to persist and mould the lives of the majority of Jews up to the present century and enabled the rabbis to come to terms with the loss of their temple, city, and land. As we have seen, protests in various forms against exile did not cease. Lurianic kabbalah, for example, was a magnificent attempt to confront the curse of exile, and Sabbatianism in its historical context can be regarded as a desperate lunge at seizing the Kingdom of God which would lead to a return to Eretz Israel. But widely, both in Orthodox Judaism (by which is here meant the main stream of Rabbinic Judaism) and in Reform Judaism in the United States and Western Europe, the question of the Land was eschatologically postponed either as an unacknowledged embarrassment or as a last or ultimate hope. Across the centuries most Jews have lived on the whims of the Gentile world: they have not been able to afford the risk of alienating their Gentile masters by giving practical expression to their visions of a territorial return to Eretz Israel. For most Jews, despite some brilliant exceptions, such visions were a luxury of Sabbath reading, dreams to be indulged in but not actively realized in daily life (Scholem 1973, n9). Instead, the rabbis emphasized that the Torah itself was to become a "portable land" for Jews: it could be obeyed everywhere and would constitute the center of Jewish religious identity everywhere.* Generally, Orthodox Judaism refused to indulge in political speculation and activity that might further a return to the Land, but accepted instead an attitude of quietism. In one of the paradoxes of history, rabbis and apocalyptists were here at one: they both preferred to wait for a divine intervention, usually postponed to an indefinite future, to produce the return (see Daube 1972, 85–86). From a different point of view, Reform Judaism, in order to accommodate its faith to the nineteenth century and to make it comparable and compatible with Christianity, also refused to give to any particular place, "the Land," a special overwhelming significance. In brief, in most rabbinic writers up to the twentieth century and in some orthodox circles even up to the present, the significance of the Land, though never denied, has been transferred to the "end of days." Paradoxically the Land retained its geographic character or actuality and was not always transcendentalized, though it was largely *de facto* removed from the realm of history altogether. And in the Reform, the Land, again in some circles even up to recent times, was conveniently relegated to a secondary place; its geographic actuality was either sublimated or transformed into a symbol of an ideal society located not necessarily in Eretz Israel. Historically then, out of necessity since 70 C.E., the doctrine of the Land as a communal concern (it was often cherished by individual Jews) was largely dormant or suffered a benign neglect in much of Judaism.

What happened is apparent. In their realism the rabbis at Jamnia had triumphed over the zealots of Masada. They recognized that the power of Rome was invincible: for them Jewish survival lay in sensible, because

---

* The phrase "portable land" comes from Louis Finkelstein. The Talmud is sometimes called a "portable state."

unavoidable, political submission, and in obedience to the Torah in all aspects of life where this was possible. The law of the country where Jews dwelt became Law. (The principle was *dina d<sup>e</sup>malkwta' dîna'*. See T. B. Nedarim 28a; T. B. Gittin 10b; T. B. Baba Kamma 113aOb; T. B. Baba Bathra 54b.) The paradigmatic figure was Johannan ben Zakkai, who had only asked of Vespasian permission to found a school where he could teach and establish a house of prayer and perform all the commandments—a spiritual center that accepted political powerlessness. For most of the rabbis after 70 C.E., exile became an accepted condition. For them discretion became the better part of valor. That it is to their discretion that Judaism owes its existence since 70 C.E. can hardly be gainsaid.

In the fourth place, exile itself is a factor that needs emphasis. David Vital begins his work *The Origins of Zionism* with the sentence, "The distinguishing characteristic of the Jews has been their Exile." Bickerman writes of the dispersion as follows:

> the post-biblical period of Jewish history, that is, that following Nehemiah . . . is marked by a unique and rewarding polarity: on the one hand, the Jerusalem center, and on the other, the plurality of centers in the Diaspora. The Dispersion saved Judaism from physical extirpation and spiritual inbreeding. Palestine united the dispersed members of the nation and gave them a sense of oneness. This counterpoise of historical forces is without analogy in antiquity. . . . The Jewish Dispersion continued to consider Jerusalem as the "metropolis" (Philo), turned to the Holy Land for guidance, and in turn, determined the destinies of its inhabitants. [Hadas 1962, 3f.]

The fact of exile has been inescapable and extraordinarily tenacious and creative in the history of Judaism. The Talmud itself, like much of the Tanak, was formulated outside the Land. Surprisingly, Judaism did not produce a theology of exile on any developed scale until late. (See now, however, Thomas M. Raitt, *A Theology of Exile, Judgement and Deliverance in Jeremiah and Ezekiel* [Philadelphia, 1977], who finds this theme developed in the Tanak.) But the presence of large bodies of Jews outside the Land, so that (until the twentieth century) the exiles became numerically and otherwise more significant than those who were in the Land, cannot but have diminished among many Jews the centrality of the Land and influenced their attitudes toward the doctrine concerning it. The conspicuous preeminence of the state of Israel in our time can easily hide the significance of the exile for Judaism throughout most of its history. But the theological preeminence of Jews outside the Land in Jewish history needs no documentation. Apart from all else, their significance in the very survival of Judaism must be recognized. The loss of the Temple and the Land, the centers of Judaism, could be sustained only because there were organized Jewish communities scattered elsewhere (G. Cohen 1961, 52). Disaster even at the center did not spell the end of Judaism but was offset and cushioned by its existence elsewhere. From this point of view, exile may be regarded as having been the historical condition for the survival of Judaism and Jewry. That this did not mean a radical decline of the significance of the primary center we shall indicate later (Vital 1975, 1–20).

The four factors we have isolated above are to be further connected with what, in a previous study, we called cautionary considerations— the possible place of the "desert" as opposed to the "Land" in Judaism, the secondary role played by Abraham outside the Pentateuch, the transcendentalizing of the Land (pointing to a muted role for it)—which tend to curb the temptation to an excessive emphasis on the territorial dimension of Judaism. We refer the reader to that study. All these factors cannot be ignored (Davies, 1974, 75–158).

## A Contradiction Resolved: The Jews' Interpretation of Their Own History

Our treatment so far has pinpointed what appears to be a contradiction: the theology of Judaism in the main seems to point to the Land as its essence; the history of Judaism seems to offer serious qualifications of this. Can the contradiction between the theology of Judaism and the actualities of its history be resolved? We suggest that the Jews' understanding of their own history comes to terms precisely with this contradiction and resolves it in life, *solvitur ambulando*. What does this mean?

On previous pages we appealed to history in support of the claim that exile as much as, if not more than, life in the Land has significantly marked Jewish history. The force of that appeal must not be belittled. In isolation, however, it is misleading, because in the Jewish experience, both religious and secular, exile has always coexisted with the hope of a

return to the Land. Without that hope the Jewish people would probably have gradually disintegrated and ceased to be. They have endured
largely because of the strength of that hope. Here the distinction between exile and simple dispersion is important: the two terms are easily
confused. Statistics cannot be supplied, but many Jews throughout the
centuries have *chosen* to live outside the Land voluntarily, and many still
do. The dispersion as such is not exile. But in most periods, Jews have
had no choice and ultimately owe their place in the various countries of
the world to the enforced exile of their ancestors. It is with these exiles,
not simply with the dispersed, that we are here concerned. This notion
of exile must be given its full weight and significance. That Jews outside
Palestine conceived of their existence as exiles meant that they were still
bound to their home base, to Eretz-Israel, wherever they were: they
were not simply dispersed. G. Cohen has urged that this was the fundamental reason that made possible the continuance of the link between
dispersed Jews and Eretz Israel. The Diaspora had maintained the notion of its existence as a *galuth,* exile. "That is to say, by the time Palestine ceased to be the central Jewish community, its centrality had been
so impressed upon the Jewish mind that it could not be uprooted"
(G. Cohen 1961, 48). Many Jews have been sustained largely by the way
in which they have traditionally interpreted their own history as revealing a recurring pattern of exile and return. They have understood their
existence (in the various countries of their abode) as essentially tran-
sients or pilgrims; they have recognized that they have had no abiding
country anywhere but have always been en route to the Land.

The Scriptures point to the patriarchs in search of the Land; the
settlement of the Land is followed by the descent (a necessary "exile")
into Egypt, followed by a return and the reconquest of the Land. Later
there is another exile to Babylon, and again a return in the time of
Cyrus. The Hellenistic period saw the rise of a vast dispersion—both
voluntary and forced—and the first century revolt against Rome was
followed by an exile that continued to this century, again only to lead to
a return. The pattern of exile and return, loss and restoration, is constant across the sweep of Jewish history. Even the so-called Non-Exilic
exile of Jews in Moorish and Christian Spain, where Jews had long enjoyed virtual integration into the societies in which they lived, ended in
disaster and a fresh dispersion. Jews have constantly been conditioned

by the harsh actualities and interpretation of their history to think of
the return. The point is that the pattern of exile and return has been
historically so inescapable that it has nurtured and underlined the belief
that there is an inseverable connection between Yahweh, his people, and
his land. In Judaism, history has reinforced theology to deepen the consciousness of Jews that the Land was always "there"—whether to be
wrestled with in occupation or to return to from exile. As Professor Edmund Jacob has written, "En effet, toute l'histoire d'Israël peut être en-
visagée comme une lutte pour la terre et avec la terre, comme le combat
de Jacob était une lutte avec Dieu and pour Dieu (Jacob 1968, 22).

In Jewish tradition the return could be conceived of in two ways. Nonreligious Jews in every age could interpret the return to the Land as a
political event, that is, as the restoration to Jews of political rights in
their own land denied them after the collapse of the Jewish revolt in
70 C.E. (unrealistic as it must have often seemed to non-Jews). Such Jews
have often understood *exile* and *return* in secular-political-economic
terms. Not only secular Jews but also many of the Sages thought of the
return in that way. The rabbinical leaders never recognized that the conquest of Eretz Israel by any foreign power could be legitimized: the Romans were usurpers, their agents thieves. The Land belonged to Israel
because Yahweh had promised it to her: her right to it was inalienable.
So in the Mishnah it is regarded as legitimate to evade the Roman taxes
(Mishnah Nedarim 3 : 4). The ruling powers were to be given obedience,
but not cooperation—even in the interest of law and order. To the rabbis
the return would involve control of the Land.

But to religious Jews much more was involved than this. To put it
simply, to them just as exile was conceived of as the outcome of the
wrath of God on a disobedient people, so too the return was to be the
manifestation of his gracious purpose for them despite their past disobedience. From this point of view the return was to be a Redemption.
What was primarily if not always exclusively of political significance to
nonreligious Jews was of theological significance for the religious Jews.

This neat division between the religious and nonreligious Jews, like all
such divisions, is misleading. Both categories were not so distinct; they
interacted and were mutually stimulating as well as quite variegated.
The concepts of the one permeated those of the other to make for in-
finite complexity. The secular thought in terms of return, and the reli-

gious in terms of Redemption ultimately, but because of the nature of the Tanak, the secular (or political) and the religious return and Redemption often dissolved into each other. In the Zionist movement, secular, socialistic Jews constantly found themselves at home with the religious members in the movement, who did not share their political views but provided a common ambience of thought on or sentiment for the Land.

Nevertheless, seeing the return in terms of Redemption had certain discernible and definite consequences, as had seeing it in terms of the restoration of political rights. To the religious Jews, as previously indicated, the various exiles the Jewish people had endured were due to the will of God. He had intervened in history to punish by exile those disobedient to the commandments. So too, they argued, the return would be an act of divine intervention. The return would be an important aspect of the messianic Redemption. As such it could not be engineered or inaugurated by political or any other human means: to force the coming of the return would be impious (see Urbach, Vol. I, 649–92). They best served that coming who waited in obedience for it: men of violence would not avail to bring it in. The rabbinic aloofness to messianic claimants sprang not only from the history of disillusionment with such but from this underlying, deeply engrained attitude. It has been claimed that under the rabbis Judaism condemned itself to powerlessness. But if such phraseology be used, it has also to be admitted that that powerlessness was effective in preserving Judaism in a hostile Christendom and must, therefore, have had its own brand of power. And there is more. Orthodoxy did recognize the dependence of the return upon the divine initiative, but this did not prevent it from always retaining in principle that a certain human obedience could bring that initiative into play. And in Lurianic Kabbala, for example, this connection was particularly active (Scholem 1973, 15–22), as in Rabbi Kuk (see Agus, 1946).

For the purpose of this essay, the significance of the attitude toward their existence in foreign lands and toward the hope of the return that I have ascribed to religious Jews is that despite their apparent quietism in the acceptance of the Torah as a portable land—and this is only an *Interimsethik*—the hope for the return to Eretz Israel never vanished from their consciousness. They remained true in spirit to the territorial theology of the Tanak and of the other sources of their faith. Religious Jews generally, especially of the most traditionalist persuasion (except perhaps in modern Germany where they often thought themselves to have been "at home"), have regarded any existing, present condition outside the Law as temporary. If not always pilgrims to it in a literal sense, they have always set their face toward the Land. This fidelity has in turn strengthened the continuing belief in the umbilical, eternal connection between the people of Israel and its Land and lent to that Land a sacred quality. In the experience of Jews, theology has informed the interpretation of history and history in turn has confirmed the theology.

In reflecting on the answer finally to be given to the question presented to us, in the light of the evidence set forth here, an analogy from Christian ecclesiology suggests itself. In Roman Catholicism and High Church Anglicanism the distinction has often been drawn, in discussions of the apostolic episcopate, between what is the *esse* and the *bene esse* of the Christian Church. Is this distinction applicable to the way in which the mainstream of Judaism has conceived of the Land? Judaism has certainly been compelled by the actualities of history to accept exile as a permanent and major mark of its existence and as a source of incalculable benefit. Has it implicitly recognized, despite the witness of its classical sources and, it might be argued, in conformity with much in them, that while life in the Land is the *bene esse* of all Jewish religious existence, it is not the *esse?* Moses desired to be in the Land so that he might have the possibility of achieving greater obedience to the Torah: that he did not enter was a great deprivation. But it was not fatal to his existence as a Jew. It is the greatest blessing to live in the Land, but living there is not absolutely essential. A Jew can remain true to his Judaism by the standards set by the sources as long as he is loyal to the Torah. He can continue in his faith outside the Land, but not outside the Torah. Not the Land but the Torah is the essence of Judaism; it is, indeed, its relation to the Torah that gives holiness to the Land. From this point of view it could be argued that the Land is the *bene esse,* not the *esse* of the Jewish faith.

Yet one is uneasy with this analogy, and not only because the Torah itself and the Mishnah are so overwhelmingly concerned with the Land. The antithesis between *esse* and *bene esse,* conceptually valid as it may seem to be, does not do justice to the place of the Land. We suggest that the way in which the question of the Land was posed at the beginning of this essay, that is, in terms of the essential in Judaism, may in fact itself be misleading and result in a misplacement in our answer. Because the term *essence* suggests the impersonal, it is as inadequate in dealing with the Land as it is in dealing with Christianity, as inadequate, for example, as Harnack's use of the notion of the "Essence of Christianity" (see Sykes 1971, vol 7). Néher and Lacocque have pointed us to the personification of the Land in Judaism (Néher 1962; Lacocque 1966). They go too far in ascribing an actual personalism to simile and metaphor and figurative language. But exaggerated as their claims may be, they do guard against impersonalism in understanding the role of the Land. The Land evokes immense and deep emotion among religious Jews: it is "La Terre mystique de l'Absolu." It presents a personal challenge and offers a personal anchorage. The sentiment (a term here used in its strict psychological sense) for the Land is so endemic among religious Jews and so constantly reinforced by their sacred sources, liturgies, and observances that to set life in the Land against life outside the Land as *esse* against *bene esse* is to miss the point. It is better to put the question in another way and ask: does the Land lie at the heart of Judaism? Put in this more personal manner the question answers itself.

Another study has suggested that for Paul as for many in early Christianity, life under the Torah and in the Land was transformed into life in Christ, which became the Christian counterpart of the life in the Land of Judaism. Few would not agree that the heart of Christianity (I avoid the term *essence*) is Jesus Christ. Similarly, we must acknowledge the heart of Judaism to be the Torah. But to accept Judaism on its own terms is to recognize that near to and indeed within that heart is the Land. In this sense, just as Christians recognize the scandal of particularity in the Incarnation, in Christ, so there is a scandal of territorial particularity in Judaism. The Land is so embedded in the heart of Judaism, the Torah, that—so its sources, worship, and theology attest—it is finally inseparable from it. "Il ne faut pas séparer les choses insepérables" (Moore 1927–30, vol. 1, 234).

The scandal presented by a particular land is no less to be recognized than that provided by a particular person. One may interpret the relation between Israel and the Land as a theological mystery or reject it simply as an unusually bizarre and irritating phenomenon. Many will find the crass materiality of the connection between Israel and the Land offensive to their mystical or spiritual sensitivities: others will find much to satisfy them in the emphasis of Judaism on the need to express itself in tangible, material societary or communal form in the Land. Of its historicity in the Jewish consciousness or self-identity there can, in any case, be no doubt. To accept it as a fact of historical significance is not to justify it, but it is to begin to understand it, and to respect it as an aspect of Judaism's doctrine of election. "S'il y a un peuple élu, il y a aussi une terre élu" (Werblowsky 1967, 376). The discussion of the Land drives us to the mystery of Israel, that is, the eschatological purpose of God in his dealings with his people.

## Conclusion

Our treatment of the Land in Judaism is over. The various aspects of the Christian response to it are foreshadowed in the New Testament: I shall remind you of them. The data in the New Testament fall into two groups.

First, there are strata in the tradition in which the Jewish understanding of the Land emerges in a critical or negative light. In one stratum (Acts 7) it was rejected outright. In other strata, the Land is taken up into a nongeographic, spiritual, transcendent dimension. It becomes a symbol especially of eternal life, of the eschatological society in time and eternity, beyond space and sense. In such strata the physical entities as such—the Land, Jerusalem, the Temple—cease to be significant, except as types of realities that are not in essence physical. It is justifiable to speak of the realia of Judaism as being spiritualized in the Christian dispensation.

But second, there are other strata in which the Land, the Temple, and Jerusalem, in their physical actuality, are regarded positively; that is, in a certain way they retain a significance in Christianity. This arises from two factors—history and theology. The emergence of the Gospels witnesses to a historical and therefore geographic concern in the tradition, which retains for the Land its full physical significance. The need to remember the Jesus of history entailed the need to remember the Jesus of a particular land. Jesus belonged not only to time, but to space; and the space and places that he occupied took on significance, so that the Land continued as a concern in Christianity. History in the tradition demanded geography.

But a theological factor also helped to ensure this. Especially in the

Fourth Gospel, the doctrine that the Word became flesh, though it resulted in a critique of distinct, traditional holy spaces, demanded the
recognition that where the glory had appeared among men all physical
forms became suffused with it. "We beheld his glory" had the corollary
that *where* this had happened became significant. If we allow a diffused
Platonic as well as apocalyptic dimension to Hebrews and the Fourth
Gospel, then their authors believe in a sacramental process, that is, the
process of reaching the truth by the frank acceptance of the actual
physical conditions of life and making these a "gate to heaven." Such
sacramentalism could find holy space everywhere, but especially where
Jesus had been. This sacramentalism was later to inform the devotion to
the holy places among many Christians throughout the ages.

The witness of the New Testament is, therefore, twofold. It transcends
the Land, Jerusalem, the Temple. But its history and theology demand a
concern with these realities also. Is there a reconciling principle between these apparently contradictory attitudes? There is. By implication, it has already been suggested. The New Testament finds holy space
wherever Christ is or has been: it personalizes "holy space" in Christ,
who, as a figure of history, is rooted in the Land; he cleansed the Temple
and died in Jerusalem, and lends his glory to these and to the places
where he was, but, as living Lord, he is also free to move wherever he
wills. To do justice to the personalism of the New Testament, that is, to
its Christocentrism, is to find the clue to the various strata of tradition
that we have traced and to the attitudes they reveal: to their freedom
from space and their attachment to holy places.

It is these attitudes, negatively and positively, that have informed the
history of Christianity. Acceptance of the doctrine of the Land, rejection, spiritualization, historical concern, sacramental concentration—
all have emerged in that history. I illustrate with a brevity that is distorting. Much modern theology, concentrating on demythologizing, tends
to reject the realia of which we speak as anachronistic; medieval and
much Puritan thought witness to their spiritualization; especially the
archaeological intensity of much modern scholarship and much also of
its literary criticism point to a historical concern centering in the quest
of the historical Jesus; and in Greek Orthodoxy and in medieval theology, expressed in the history of pilgrimages to Palestine and in the
Crusades, connected as these are with the motif of the imitation of

Christ, the sacramentalism of which I spoke is a striking characteristic. To illustrate all this in depth is beyond the range of this lecture. But one thing in the history of Christianity—I do not say Christendom—needs no illustration, so ubiquitous is it: its Christocentrism. In the end, where Christianity has reacted seriously to the realia of Judaism, whether negatively or positively, it has done so in terms of Christ, to whom all places and all space, like all things else, are subordinated.

In sum, for the holiness of place, Christianity has fundamentally, though not consistently, substituted the holiness of the person: it has Christified holy space. I suggested elsewhere that to be "in Christ" for Christians is to be "in the Land."

## Literature Cited

Agus, J. B. *Banner of Jerusalem. The Life, Time and Thought of Abraham Isaac Kuk.* New York, 1946.

Brody, H., ed. *Selected Poems of Jehudah Halevi.* Translated by Nina Salaman. Philadelphia, 1946.

Cohen, G. In *Zion in Jewish Literature,* edited by G. S. Halkin. New York, 1961.

Cohen, H. *Religion der Vernuft aus den Quellen des Judentums.* Translated by Simon Kaplan. New York, 1972.

Davis, W. D. *The Setting of the Sermon on the Mount.* Cambridge, 1964.

———. *The Gospel and the Land: Early Christianity and Jewish Territorial Doctrine.* Berkeley, 1974.

———. "From Schweitzer to Scholem: Reflections on Sabbatai Svi." *Journal of Biblical Literature* 95 (1976): 529–58.

Daube, David. *Civil Disobedience in Antiquity.* Edinburgh, 1972.

Hadas, M., trans. *From Ezra to the Last of the Maccabees.* Foundations of Post-Biblical Judaism, part 2. New York, 1962.

Jacob, Edmund. *Israël dans la perspective biblique.* Strabourg, 1968.

Klein, G. *Anti-Judaism in Christian Theology.* Philadelphia, 1975.

Lacocque, A. "Une Terre qui decoule de Lait et de Miel." *Revue du Dialogue* no. 2 (1966): 28–36.

Lieberman, S. *Proceedings of the Rabbinical Assembly of America.* Vol. 12. New York, 1949.

Marquardt, F. W. *Die Juden und ihr Land.* Hamburg, 1975.

Moore, G. F. *Judaism in the First Centuries of the Christian Era: The Age of the Tannaim.* 3 vols. Cambridge, Mass., 1927–30.

Néher, A. "Israel, terre mystique de l'Absolu." In *L'Existence Juive*. Paris, 1962.

Neusner, J. *The Journal of Religion* 59 (1979): 71–86.

Noth, M. *History of Israel*. London, 1958.

Scholem, Gershom. *Sabbatai Svi: The Mystic Messiah, 1626–1676*. Princeton, 1973.

*Jews and Judaism in Crisis*. New York, 1976.

Stern, M. *Greek and Latin Authors on Jews and Judaism*. Jerusalem, 1974.

Sykes, S. W. In *Religious Studies*. Cambridge, 1971.

Urbach, E. E. *The Sages*. 2 vols. Jerusalem, 1975.

Vital, David. *The Origins of Zionism*. Oxford, 1975.

Werblowsky, R. J. Zwi. "Israel et Eretz Israel." *Les Temps Modernes* no. 253, B15 (1967): 371–93.

# The Idea of a People of God

JOHN MACQUARRIE

ONE OF THE MOST typical ideas in the Judeo-Christian tradition, equally important in both the Jewish and Christian branches, is that of a people of God. Israel is the elect of God, the people he has formed for himself; they will be his people and he will be their God (Isa. 42:1; 62:12). Likewise, the Christian Church has believed itself to be a chosen generation, a royal priesthood, a holy nation, a peculiar people (1 Pet. 2:9).

Is this idea of a people of God a restrictive, separatist, elitist idea? Does it lead to an exclusiveness and sense of superiority on the part of those who think of themselves as belonging to the elect people? It has sometimes been alleged that the Judeo-Christian tradition has been more intolerant than some of the East Asian religious traditions, for example. It may indeed be the case that the idea of a people of God has sometimes been interpreted along exclusivist lines, but this need not be the case, and it has not been the case in those moments of deepest insight among those who have thought of themselves as the people of God. The very use of the word *people* in the expression "people of God" is highly significant. It indicates a connection with a human reality, and because of this the expression relates somehow to all people, to humanity as such. In what it had to say about the Church, the Second Vatican Council made the idea of a people of God fundamental. Because of this, it was able to present a far more open view than was possible when the understanding of the Church was presented under more restrictive images, such as "the Body of Christ" or, even more, the ark of salvation floating upon the stormy waters. These two images, especially the second, tended to stress the discontinuity of the Church with the world around, whereas the image of the people of God tends to stress continuity with the whole human race, even with people of other faiths.

It is not only the word *people* that broadens the reference, for the broadening is carried even further by the use of the word *God*. A universal reference is hidden in the word, for God is believed to be the author and ruler of all. One of the most central teachings in the Judeo-Christian tradition is the doctrine of creation. According to this teaching, the whole universe, including the entire human race, are creatures of God, and this can only mean that, at least ideally, the entire human race is the people of God.

Let us consider a little more closely this expression, "the people of God." Superficially, it appears to be a descriptive phrase, similar, let us say, to "the people of Mexico," "the people of the Stone Age," "the people of the Amazon basin," and so on. But the resemblance is only superficial, for when we say, "the people *of God*," we introduce a new dimension of meaning that sets this phrase apart from the others. The other phrases are simply factual descriptions of groups of human beings, distinguished by the circumstance that they share a common citizenship or lived during a particular epoch or are found in a certain geographical area, but the expression "people of God" neither can nor does function in any such way. "The people of God" is a typical piece of religious language. The word *people*—meaning a group of human beings, perhaps a nation or some other more or less clearly defined segment or community—is an ordinary empirical reference to something within our ordinary range of experience, people who can be seen and heard, loved or hated, admired or despised, people who have a share in shaping the history of our planet. But where the phrase differs from any ordinary description is in its use of the words *of God*. This people is not defined by any empirical characteristics, such as citizenship, language, ethnic inheritance, cultural peculiarities, or anything of the sort. Any or all of these may be present in varying degrees, but they are not defining characteristics. This people is defined as being "of God"—elect of God, belonging to God, summoned by God, sanctified of God, perhaps even alienated from God, but always defined by the relation to God. But God is not an empirical phenomenon within the world. The expression, "the people of God," is a typical piece of religious language because it takes an empirical concept, namely people, and by relating it to the key word of all religion, God, transforms it into a transempirical concept. This people is to be seen in a new dimension of depth, in a new set of relations that lie beyond those discoverable by empirical observation. To explore further what this means will be one of our main tasks.

A good starting point for this exploration is the cycle of stories in Genesis relating to Abraham. He is often called the first man of faith, though from the beginning Abraham appears not just as an individual but as the leader and representative of a community. The ancient stories of Abraham's journeys and adventures do not introduce explicitly those modern sophisticated philosophical problems on which I have just touched—problems about the use of language, the theory of descriptions, the question of empirical verification and the like—but they do show an astonishing insight into the nature and destiny of the human race as it strives to become a true people of God. In that cycle of Abraham stories there is already contained *in nuce* most of the fundamental themes that were to be unfolded in the subsequent development of the Judeo-Christian tradition, and, not least among them, the theme of a people of God.

The first story in the Abraham saga tells of his departure from the city of Haran in Mesopotamia (Gen. 12:1–9). The history of the people of God begins with an act of separation, which is necessary in order to establish an identity. No doubt Abraham had been successful enough in Haran; he seems to have been a man of substance. But he found no true contentment in that affluent society. He was ready to move on to something else, and something better, even if he did not quite know what it would be. He was ready, we could say, for the voice of God and the summons to a new life. We are told that he heard the divine voice commanding him, "Get thee out of thy country, and from thy kindred, and from thy father's house, unto a land that I will show thee." But it was not just a command that the voice spoke; it was also a promise. "I will make of thee a great nation, and I will bless thee, and make thy name great; and thou shalt be a blessing . . . and in thee shall all families of the earth be blessed." These few verses are laden with profound meaning. The people of God has been from the beginning a dynamic people, a people on the move, unable to settle down, both driven by a divine discontent and drawn by a divine promise. This indeed implies separation from and departure out of the environing society. The people of God could never have been born if Abraham and his companions had been content to stay part of Mesopotamian society, had continued to accept its standards and follow its customs, and had never looked beyond its mode of life. Abraham turned his back on that settled society and headed into the wilderness of the south—the wilderness where the land was still virgin and had not yet been given shape, and where a new society could be built on principles different from those that governed the old. It is a picture that ought to have a special appeal to Americans, whose forefathers turned their backs on Europe to risk everything for the sake of building a new society in a virgin land. Abraham's separation was necessary, but it must have been painful, and we must note that from the beginning the separation was never conceived as a sheer abandonment. The promise was that through Abraham all the families of the earth would find blessing, and this would include the families that he had left behind in Haran.

The people of God exists in a dialectical relation to the human race at large. To become the people of God requires a distinctive existence if that people is to serve any purpose at all. Yet, the people of God remain linked at a deep level to the human race as a whole and will eventually prove a blessing to all.

We could go further, and say that this story about the beginning of the people of God is a parable of the situation of the whole human race. The entire race is on a pilgrimage into the wilderness of the unknown, in search of a true humanity and a true community. The entire race is summoned to set out from where it is at any given time in quest of something new and better, stirred by divine discontent and drawn by divine promise, even if these are often suppressed and forgotten. For it is all too easy for human beings to settle down where they are, to evade the labors and anxieties of pilgrimage, to be content with the familiar and to seek to establish what is intended to be an enduring, unchanging order. That is why a special people of God is needed—a minority who will not stay put but will insist on going on to something new and better, yet not for themselves alone but for the ultimate blessing of all.

The next story in the Abraham saga is a sharp rebuke to any who might suppose that the people of God is a superior elite, impervious to the sins and temptations of ordinary mortals (Gen. 12:14–20). There was a famine, and Abraham went down to Egypt in search of sustenance. But he was anxious about what might happen to him there. In particular, because his wife Sarah was a woman of great beauty, he was afraid that some Egyptian potentate might have him killed in order to take possession of his wife. So he practiced a deception. He pretended that Sarah was his sister and let her be taken into the harem of the king of Egypt, while he himself received generous gifts from the king in return for the favor he had shown him. Even in those ancient times (or, especially in those ancient times), Abraham's action was regarded as mean, sordid, and shameful. But the story was not suppressed when Israel's historians came to write up the chronicles of the people. It was allowed to stand in the record, near the beginning of the epic of God's people. It is a perpetual reminder that there is neither instant perfection nor automatic progress in the life of the people of God. Indeed, the very possibility of progress means that there must also be the possibility of regress, and as a matter of historical fact, the people of God, whether in its Jewish or its Christian manifestation, has had many backslidings. Not seldom its leaders have manifested less integrity than pagans and secularists, just as Abraham did in his dealings with the king of Egypt.

There is another remarkable story that speaks plainly of the continuing solidarity between the people of God and the rest of the human race (Gen. 18:16–23). Indeed, it expresses in story form something that remains a mystery even for our most sophisticated philosophies of human nature, namely, that there are hidden but nonetheless powerful ties that bind all mankind in a single bundle of life. Abraham's companion, Lot, who had been one of the company that departed from Haran and therefore himself one of the people of God, had separated himself from Abraham. He had perhaps found the demands of the new life more than he had expected and longed for the urban comforts that he had known in Haran. So he had chosen for himself and his flocks the most fertile part of the land in the vicinity of the cities of Sodom and Gomorrah, while Abraham sojourned in the wilderness country toward the south. It would not be unfair to say that Lot had lapsed back into the old life, that he had become an apostate and had fallen away from his vocation to the people of God. Abraham himself could have had no sympathy with him. Indeed, Lot's action was threatening the very existence of the new community as it struggled for survival. Abraham must have had even less sympathy with Lot's new associates, the people of Sodom and Gomorrah. These cities represented the worst of the kind of life that Abraham was trying to leave behind. They were a byword for the life of luxury, self-indulgence, materialism, hedonism, vice. Yet when Lot was taken prisoner by some invading armies, it was Abraham who went to his rescue. What is even more remarkable, when the Lord was determined to destroy the cities of the plain for their wickedness, it was Abraham who interceded for them. There are few more poignant passages in the Bible than Abraham's pleading before God for Sodom and Gomorrah—if there are fifty righteous people in these cities, spare them; if there are forty-five, forty, thirty, twenty, ten. . . . What is the meaning of this prayer? It certainly refutes any accusation that the elect people had turned its back on mankind and was concerned only for itself. What we have here is the remarkable dialectic of separation and solidarity, characteristic of the people's life. There had to be separation. The chosen people had to distance itself, sometimes in prophetic denunciation, from whatever marred and destroyed the truly human quality of life. But deeper than the separation is the solidarity, the kinship with all fellow human beings, who are also potentially the people of God even if they have turned away from their true destiny and there is hardly a trace of righteousness to be found among them.

We cannot explore all the Abraham stories, instructive though they are, but there is one more that cannot be ignored, for it is both the best known and the most difficult of all—the story of how the divine voice commands Abraham to sacrifice his only son, Isaac, and of how Abraham demonstrated his willingness to obey even this terrible command (Gen. 22:1–14). In a famous discussion of this incident, Søren Kierkegaard claimed that there are moments in life when a higher obligation demands that we set aside the ordinary claims of morality and of natural affection in order to obey the higher claim. It may be questioned whether Kierkegaard was entirely successful in his attempt to interpret the story, though it must also be remembered that at the end of the day the sacrifice of Isaac was not required and that God himself provided a sacrifice in Isaac's place. But whatever argument there might be over the details of this story, some points seem to be clear enough. The way of the people of God will be a costly way, one of struggle and suffering and sacrifice. It will not be a way of privilege and triumph. Yet there is also the assurance that the people are not alone in their suffering and sacrifice: God is with them; he even shares their suffering and provides their sacrifices. One is reminded of the recurring phrase "the pathos of God" in Abraham Heschel's writings about Israel.

How these thoughts 'were developed in the prophetic tradition of Israel is well known. That tradition culminates in the idea of the suffering servant, despised and rejected by men yet charged with a mission to the nations and upheld by God (Isa. 45:1–4, 53). And this prophetic vision was no mere idea, but has been concrete in the actual historical sufferings of Israel, not only those recorded in the Bible but those that have followed down to the present day. And who can doubt that these have also been the sufferings and sacrifices of God? In the words of a late prophet, "In all their afflictions, he was afflicted" (Isa. 63:9).*

As I mentioned, all the essential characteristics of the people of God are already presented in symbolic or narrative form in the Abraham cycle of stories. These characteristics all reappear in the Christian Church, which has also claimed to be a people of God, and which, in its being and history, has shown many remarkable parallels with Israel. There has been the same dialectic of separation and solidarity. The Church could only come into being by asserting its distinctiveness from Israel. For the first three centuries of its existence it lived on the margin of society, cut off from the mainstream of life in the Roman Empire, a suspect and often persecuted sect. Yet even at that time, within the Church, there was taking place a remarkable breaking down of barriers between social and ethnic groups, and there was emerging a new sense of human solidarity. Again, like Israel before it, the Church had many backslidings, and there have been many occasions when it was tempted by the triumphalism of power, forgetting that all human existence is pilgrimage and that the goal of a truly mature people of God has not yet been attained. There have been times of arrogance when the Church has sought to dominate

---

* The translation of the Hebrew is doubtful, but the translation here, following the King James version, seems to be a true reflection of the prophet's intention.

the world, forgetting the New Testament teaching that it is meant to be the leaven that leavens the whole lump, not the lump itself (Luke 13:21). The Church too has shrunk from the costliness and sacrifice that are demanded from the people of God, though in its finest hours it has remembered that its symbol is the cross, and that its greatest achievements have been purchased with the blood of its martyrs and saints. The Church, after all, is the Church of Jesus Christ; indeed, it claims to be his Body, an extension of his life of love and service. But Jesus Christ was not only the founder of the Christian community; he was also a true son of Israel, and it was this insight that led some of his earliest followers to connect him with the suffering servant of the Lord portrayed in deutero-Isaiah. That suffering servant is at one and the same time the people of Israel, Jesus Christ, and the Christian Church— they are all manifestations of the life that is defined by the relation to God.

But how can I say such a thing—that the Jewish people and the Christian Church are both manifestations of the people of God? Is this not to ignore far too blandly the tragic history of the relations between Jews and Christians—relations which, from the beginning, have been marked not so much by friendship or awareness of a common mission, as by enmities, disputes, accusations, even persecutions and overt violence? It has been a sad history. Perhaps Christians must especially confess this, since Christians have so often been in the majority and have been the instigators of persecution. Yet in such matters no group ever has a monopoly of sin. The separation in the earliest period of the new Christian sect from its Jewish matrix was the necessary consequence of the dialectical existence of a people of God. The tragedy was that only one side of the dialectic—separation—was allowed to come into play, while the other side—solidarity—disappeared from view. Perhaps Paul, himself schooled in the best traditions of Judaism, had a vision of the eventual reconciliation of Jews and Christians, but this was not taken up by his fellow Christians (Rom. 10 and 11).

We must hope that today we are standing at the beginning of a new era in Jewish-Christian relations. From a theological point of view, a deeper exploration by both traditions of the idea of a people of God could go far toward bringing them closer together. Surely, both the needs of mankind and the purposes of God are big enough to make room for both peoples of God, or rather, for the two manifestations of the one people, existing not in competition but in complement.

Another serious question for both groups, Jews and Christians, is how they have related, as people of God, to other human groups that do not stand in the Judeo-Christian tradition. To make this question specific, let us consider for a few moments the difficult question of the relation to Islam, for Muslims constitute the religious community that stands nearest to Jews and Christians. The religion of Islam looks back to Abraham, just as Judaism and Christianity begin with Abraham. Once again, however, we find that the relations among these three great religions have been far from friendly. The victorious armies of Islam, spilling out of the Arabian peninsula, overran the Christian provinces of North Africa and the Near East, and for a long time they threatened to conquer Europe itself by a two-pronged invasion through Spain in the west and the Balkans in the east. Christian Europe's reply was to hit back at Islam in the long and frustrating series of expeditions that we call the Crusades. In recent years, relations between Judaism and Islam have been particularly strained, and we seem to be still far removed from a solution. Yet, if Islam too looks back to Abraham, then it shares with all mankind in the promise that in Abraham all the families of the earth would be blessed. In fact, the promise is more specific even than that. While the main line of the people of God has descended from Abraham through Isaac, there was another line stemming from Ishmael, also a son of Abraham and traditionally regarded as the ancestor of those Semitic peoples whom today we call the Arabs. In that same cycle of stories about Abraham from which we have drawn so much, we find God reportedly saying to Hagar the bondwoman, concerning Ishmael, the son she had had by Abraham, "I will make him a great nation" (Gen. 21:18). So Ishmael's descendants too are a kind of people of God, and certainly they belong, as do Hindus, Buddhists, and many others, to that ideal people of God that potentially embraces the whole race. Christians and Jews are not privileged in having been called to be people of God. They have rather been given a special and sometimes heavy responsibility. They have been entrusted with a vision the origins of which extend deeply into biblical history. In spite of suffering and discouragement, they must go on seeking the realization of that vision, until all the peoples of the earth are embraced within it in a true peace or wholeness.

We noted that the expression "people of God" has as its two main terms the words *people* and *God*. We have been thinking principally of the first of these and considering the role of a people of God as an agent of peace and reconciliation among the nations of the earth. But now we must turn to the other term, *God*. It was this word, we said, that gives a new depth to the ordinary sense of the word *people*, that transfers it from the area of everyday discourse into that of religious language. What is the meaning of this talk of God, and what is the place of God in the life of the people? In a secularized age like ours, does it make sense to talk of God or to assign importance to him?

In order to know what the word *God* means, or, perhaps better, to know who God is, we have to glance once more over the history of the people of God and learn how he has functioned in that history. It began with Abraham's hearing an inner voice, feeling an inner constraint or obligation, experiencing a divine discontent. He could not rest with himself as he was or with society as it was, he felt himself called out of that, even driven out of it. Not what is but what ought to be became important for him. That deep sense of oughtness or obligation, the drive to go beyond the facts of the empirical situation toward the realization of an as yet distant vision, is quite fundamental to the Judeo-Christian experience of God. But the inner voice was not only command and constraint, it was also promise and hope. In a world where moral obligation has the ultimacy that the Judeo-Christian tradition has ascribed to it, there must be moral government and therefore hope for the future. Such a world view is theistic, and God is seen as the source and center of all. God, conceived in this way, is well described in the words of Matthew Arnold as "the Power not ourselves making for righteousness". It is this righteous Power operating in history that has again and again impressed itself on Jew and Christian alike, especially in those great events seen as "revelations"—so much so that they have believed that the vast universe itself has been created, sustained, and governed by such a righteous Power. Yet this is not some distant Power remote in the heavens, unaffected by the sufferings of his creatures. God is close to his creation, the fellow sufferer who is afflicted in the afflictions of his people, the crucified God who from the beginning has been pouring out his being in sacrificial love. The Judeo-Christian God is by no means an outmoded concept. Rather, this form of theism makes more sense than any other world view that is current today.

Not only does it make more sense; it supplies a dynamic of faith and hope not only for Jews and Christians but for the whole human race. There is a blessing here for all the families of earth. All humanity is seen potentially as a people of God, brought to maturity in peace and righteousness. In spite of all their failures and backslidings, those representative peoples, Israel and the Church, have labored and will continue to labor for the fulfillment of the wider vision.

## Literature Cited

Arnold, Matthew, *Literature and Dogma.*
Heschel, A.J. *The Prophets.*
Kierkegaard, Søren. *Fear and Trembling.*

# Toward a Jewish Theology of Christianity

JAKOB J. PETUCHOWSKI

IN 1971 MONSIGNOR JOHN M. OSTERREICHER wrote a little volume called *The Rediscovery of Judaism* to which I wrote the introduction. Incidentally, it is a kind of barometer of the changed theological climate in that when I was invited to write this *nihil obstat* to a Catholic's book on Judaism, I recalled the many, many centuries when Jewish books had to be submitted to Christian censors to be sure that nothing anti-Christian was contained therein. And here was John Osterreicher submitting his manuscript to me to make sure that nothing against Jews was contained in his book. Anyway, in that introduction I also included a sentence that read, "We need a Jewish theology of Christianity and a Christian theology of Judaism." This statement has been frequently quoted.

I will admit quite frankly that my statement is not without its problems. Of course, there always has been a Christian theology of Judaism: Barnabas in the second century wrote some nasty things about Judaism, and even a secularized Christian like Toynbee in the twentieth century did not have very nice things to say about Judaism, because Judaism did not fit into his scheme. You see, if the Jews had been decent, they would have politely bowed out of history or died off when Christianity came along. But since the Jews, without politeness, insisted on surviving, they have been a thorn in the theological flesh of the Church; and the Church has reacted in various negative ways. That is why, until the present time, the Christian theology of Judaism has been one with which Jews could not be particularly happy. But let us realize that Christianity definitely needs a Christian theology of Judaism, whether that be a positive or a negative one, because Christian theology needs to have an attitude toward Judaism—Christianity's only legitimization. Because the central events of Christianity are presented, and always have been presented, as the fulfilment of Jewish Scriptures, Christianity always had something to say about Judaism. What it has been saying lately, particularly after Vatican II, has been a great improvement over what it had been saying before, and I see signs of hope in both Catholic and Protestant circles, not least, for understandable reasons, in Europe generally and in West Germany particularly.

But a Jewish theology of Christianity comes up against several problems. First, Judaism draws its self-awareness, its beliefs about God, creation, revelation, and redemption from its own sources. It was there first, and it does not have to legitimize its truth or Scriptures from any other religion. The medieval poet-philosopher, Judah Halevi, wrote a philosophical treatise called the *Book of Kuzari,* which has a vague historical basis. Sometime around the eighth or ninth century the royal house of the kingdom of the Khazars in southern Russia (the Crimea) and the aristocracy—and probably a large section of the population— converted to Judaism. Judah Halevi asked himself the question, How could anybody convert to Judaism, given the rather unpleasant conditions of Jewish life at that particular time? As he recreates the event, he has the king of the Khazars dissatisfied with the pagan religion of his own ancestors, and engaging in the study of comparative religion. That is to say, he was trying out various religions. Each time he tried a new one, a heavenly voice addressed him in a dream, telling him his intentions were good, but what he was doing was bad. The king of the Khazars staged a public discussion, an ecumenical forum. He invited an Aristotelian philosopher, a Christian scholar, and a Muslim scholar. Of course, no Jew was invited, because since the Jews were suffering so much, they could not possibly have the right religion. He asked the philosopher, "What do you believe?" The philosopher presented all the traditional arguments for the existence of God. The king of the Khazars then asked, "Tell me, Mr. Philosopher, just as by reason you can prove the existence of God, could you also disprove it?" And the philosopher came up with the notion that reason could also disprove the existence of God. The king of the Khazars decided that this was not the religion for him.

He then asked the Christian scholar to prove that his religion was right. The Christian scholar answered, "My religion fulfils the prophecies of the Hebrew Bible." The king of the Khazars replied, "That is very interesting, but let us hear from our Muhammedan friend." The Muhammedan started talking about Abraham and God's covenant with Abraham, as found in the Hebrew Bible and which is manifest in the final revelation of Allah through Muhammed and the religion of Islam. I can image the king of the Khazars scratching his head as he mused, "I wonder what kind of a religion this must be, because here both the Christian and Muslim are trying to justify themselves on the basis of the Hebrew Scriptures. I had better call in a Hebrew to see what he himself has to say." It is not history the way I relate it, but it is interesting that a medieval thinker should have thought about it in this particular fashion. That is to say, other religions try to prove their truths on the basis of the Jewish Scripture. Jewish Scripture stands in and by itself. But to get back to our topic, if Christianity needs some kind of statement about Judaism to legitimatize itself, the Jewish religion needs to make no reference to Christianity in order to demonstrate its own system of beliefs. That is the first problem.

The second difficulty is that there are some Jews who do not consider theology to be a Jewish enterprise in the first place. Occasionally fellow Jews will ask me "What do you do for a living?" When I answer that I teach theology, they tell me that that is not a Jewish subject. The Jews who feel that theology is not a Jewish subject mean a theology of *Judaism;* they do not even mention a Jewish theology of Christianity. Those people are wrong. Jews may not always have theologized in the same way that Christians do. With notable exceptions in both the Middle Ages and today, Jews have avoided systematic theology and have cultivated narrative theology instead—theology by storytelling rather than by the creation of impressive theological systems. But there certainly is a Jewish theology, or more accurately perhaps, there are various Jewish theologies because Jews can never agree on anything.

The third difficulty about a Jewish theology of Christianity is that there is one sentence in the New Testament that Jews have always taken seriously, and that is Matthew 7:16: "By their fruits shall ye know them." When I was a young student rabbi, commuting eight hours on the train every second weekend to a small West Virginia community where I served for six years, I once prepared a sermon that I thought was one of my better ones. As always happens after the services, the congregation lined up and expressed their gratitude for the edification of my sermon, except old Mr. Kaufmann, who did not shake my hand but screamed, "Young man, you have no business being a rabbi!" When I wanted to know why, he answered, "Because you quoted the New Testament in your sermon." Still confused, I defended my use of the New Testament, explaining that it contained some good Jewish teachings. Not in the least appeased, Mr. Kaufmann related how he came to be in America. He had escaped to this country from Poland at the beginning of this century, fleeing a pogrom. The last thing he remembered of Poland was his family being killed by a mob; and the mob was being led by a Catholic priest, who held the crucifix high. "And that, young man," Mr. Kaufmann concluded, "is why I would thank you for not quoting the New Testament in my synagogue!" Mr. Kaufmann's story is paradigmatic of the Jewish attitude toward Christianity in those many centuries and in those many geographical locations that are associated in the Jewish mind with Christian persecutions of Jews. Jews believe that "By their fruits ye shall know them."

The creation of a Jewish theology of Christianity is going to take a while because we shall need years, perhaps centuries, of better relations between Christians and Jews before ordinary Jews who are not professional theologians will evince any interest in a Jewish theology of Christianity. But the formulation of such a theology cannot be shirked, not only because we are living in an ecumenical age, but also because any Jewish theology must say something about God, and contrary to what some people think, there are Jewish theologies. And any Jewish theology that speaks about God would sooner or later come to the affirmation that the God of Judaism is the loving Father of all humankind. We know that He revealed Himself to Israel. But what has He been doing for all His other children? The rest of humankind are God's children too. It is all very nice to hear about God's revealing Himself through

Moses and the prophets to the children of Israel, but what did He do for the rest of His children?

Attempts at answering that particular question were made in early rabbinic times. For instance, there is the story told in Siphre to Deuteronomy, paragraph 343, pages 395 to 397 in the Finkelstein edition. Before God gave the Torah to Israel, He hawked it around to all kinds of other nations; and nobody wanted it. The other nations said: "All right, God, You want to give us the Torah. What's in it?" And God said, "Thou shalt not murder." And one nation said, "We live by murder; we have no use for Your revelation." And another nation asked, "What's in Your Torah?" And God said: "Thou shalt not steal." And that nation replied: "Well, what happens to business then? The Torah is not for us." A third nation, when offered the Torah, asked God: "What's in it?" And God said: "Thou shalt not commit adultery." And they as much as said: "Sovereign of the Universe, have You never heard of the new morality by which we live? We have no use of Your Torah." Finally, almost in desperation, God picked on the children of Israel and they, not being very smart, did not first ask, "What is written in it?" But they said, "All that the Lord God has said we shall do and we shall try to understand." And the Jews got stuck with the Torah. What is important in this story is the thought, the self-awareness of the rabbis who told that story. They had to be the monotheistic minority in a pagan world. Didn't God try to do anything for the pagans? And they answered, "Yes, He tried, but He did not succeed with them as He did with us."

The second attempt to answer the question of what God has done for the rest of His children is the story of Baalam, in Siphré to Deuteronomy, paragraph 357, page 430. Baalam was an early anti-Semite, a prophet who was hired to curse the children of Israel. But he did not quite succeed; God turned the words in his mouth. When Baalam wanted to curse, out came the words "How goodly are thy tents, O Jacob, thy dwelling places, O Israel," with which all Jewish services begin. (I always point out to my students that not *all* our prayers were written by anti-Semites.) The one true God communicated with Baalam; he was a prophet. How could God do more for Baalam than He normally does for you and me? If you claim that God talks to you, some people might suggest you see a psychiatrist. But God really did talk to

Baalam, the heathen. And when, in the end of the book of Deuteronomy, Scripture says, "There arose not in Israel a prophet like Moses," the rabbis pick up that verse: In a non-Jewish nation such a prophet did arise—Baalam. That is to say, the heathen prophet equalled, if indeed he did not surpass, the prophetic gift of Moses, so that in some segments of rabbinic literature the heathen prophet Baalam takes the role of the great Apostle to the Gentiles. As far as the rabbis saw the economy of Divine Revelation, God sent Moses to Israel; God sent Baalam to the non-Jewish peoples.

A third attempt to deal with the problem is recorded in Genesis 9 : 8–17, where the Bible tells us that, after the Flood, God made a covenant with Noah and his sons; and that, of course, means a covenant with the surviving ancestors of the entire human race. We shall come back to that later.

But what about the Christians specifically? Thus far I have not been talking about Christians. I have been talking about non-Jews in general. One of the problems that should concern us is whether non-Jews and Christians are identical. This is an important question, because all the stories that I have briefly related refer to the non-Jewish world as such, not specifically Christianity. As far as Christianity is concerned, there are a couple of unpleasant chapters in past relations. I want to clarify one thing: I think that as far as Rabbinic Judaism is concerned, the distinction must be made between the attitude of Pharisaic-Rabbinic Judaism to Judeo-Christians on one hand, and the attitude of Pharisaic-Rabbinic Judaism to Gentile Christianity on the other hand.

Judeo-Christians were disliked not primarily for theological reasons, but for political reasons. This was a time of repeated attempts to throw the Romans out of Palestine. There were numerous wars of national liberation that all came to grief. Most people know of the Bar-Kokhba rebellion around 135 C.E. But that was not the only Jewish rebellion against Rome. The Christian Jews, or Jewish Christians, did not fight in the wars of national liberation because usually the generals who led those wars also made messianic claims for themselves. A Christian Jew could not enroll in the army of Bar-Kokhba, who claimed to be the Messiah, because the Christian Jew knew that the name of the Messiah was Jesus and not Bar-Kokhba. In a war of national liberation those not fighting on one side are suspected, rightly or wrongly, of making common cause with the enemy. In second-century Palestine, Christian Jews or Jewish Christians were invariably suspected of making common cause with the Roman enemy. Their identification of the Messiah with Jesus of Nazareth was not a terrible theological sin. The second-century rabbi, Akiba, one of the master builders of Pharisaic-Rabbinic Judaism, supported the messianic claims of Bar-Kokhba. But Akiba was wrong. In fact, his colleagues had already told him: "Akiba, you're wrong. Grass is going to grow through your cheeks before the true Messiah comes." But nobody has ever excommunicated Rabbi Akiba, who died a martyr's death. So the split between the Jewish Christians and the rest of the Jewish community was not a question of messianic identification, but of the practical consequences that were drawn from that messianic identification. Also, once the good Apostle Paul made inroads even within the Christian Jewish community and the Law was undermined, Jewish society felt threatened. The degree of autonomy and independence Jews experienced even in Roman-occupied Palestine was due to the fact that the Romans recognized the rule of Jewish Law for the Jewish community and the authority of the rabbis to interpret Jewish Law. The rabbis had no use for anybody who undermined the foundation of Jewish Law, whether that person believed that Jesus was the Messiah or not. Christians were not the only people who attacked the rule of Jewish Law. From the point of view of Rabbinic Judaism, the animosity toward Jewish Christians was primarily political rather than theological.

Theological differences that arose later, however, made the break final. But by contrast, theologically, Rabbinic Judaism could have a positive relation to Gentile Christians. Why? Because Rabbi Joshua, in Tosephta Sanhedrin 13 : 2, taught the great lesson that you do not have to be Jewish to go to heaven, or, as he put it, "There are righteous people among the Gentiles who have a share in the world to come." "To have a share in the world to come" is the rabbis' way of saying they will be saved. You do not have to be Jewish to enjoy Rubel's rye bread, and you do not even have to be Jewish to go to heaven. What do you have to do to go to heaven? Here we get back to Genesis 9 and the covenant that God made with Noah and his sons—not with Jews, but with the ancestors of the entire human race itself. (Tosephta 'Abhodah Zarah 8 (9): 4, ed. Zuckermandel, p. 473; b. Sanhedrin 562; Genesis Rabbah, Noah, 34, ed. Theodor-Albeck, pp. 316f.) The covenant that God made with the ancestors of the entire human race, as the rabbis understood it, was for the entire human race to abide by seven commandments:

1. prohibition of idolatry
2. prohibition of sexual immorality
3. prohibition of murder
4. prohibition of blasphemy
5. prohibition of theft
6. prohibition of cruelty to animals
7. to establish courts of justice—the one positive commandment

Any Gentile adhering to those so-called Noahite commandments was entitled to his share in the world to come just as much as the Jews, who had to adhere not to 7 commandments, but to 613.

We in academic circles, and even those of us who only watch movies of the Hellenistic-Roman period, can easily understand that a pagan in that Roman world who converted to Christianity had a greater chance of being recognized among the righteous of the Gentile world than did the pagan who did not convert. And if you read Acts 15 carefully, you will find that the admission requirements of the Church were based largely on what the rabbis had outlined for the sons of Noah. Therefore, any animosity that the rabbis felt toward Jewish Christians was unnecessary as far as Gentile Christianity was concerned, at least as a theoretical possibility. Whether this theoretical possibility was practically acknowledged by the rabbis is another question again. Gentile Christians gave the rabbis a rough time theologically. They claimed that God had rejected the Jews, that the Jews did not understand their own Scriptures, that the Law had been abolished. Refuting all those arguments, the rabbis may have had neither time nor inclination to welcome those Gentile Christians as "righteous persons among the Gentile nations." But what the rabbis of the first six centuries might have omitted to do, later rabbis of the thirteenth, fourteenth, and fifteenth centuries did explicitly acknowledge. Those rabbis argued that the Christians in Europe, among whom they lived, were to be technically considered as righteous persons among the Gentiles, adhering to the Seven Laws of the Sons of Noah, and, therefore, being part of the covenant that God made with Noah and his sons.

Now this, however, does not yet represent the Jewish theology of Christianity. Any righteous Gentile, not only a Christian but a Muslim, a Buddhist, a Taoist, or, we may say, even possibly an atheist or a Marxist might qualify for status as one who has a share in the world to come by not murdering, fornicating, stealing, being cruel to animals, and so on. In other words, the concept of the righteous person among the Gentiles in and by itself does not imply any special affinity of Jews to Christianity nor any recognition that Christianity is closer to the Jewish religion than other religions. But Moses Maimonides in the twelfth century did view Christianity, and Islam for that matter, from the Jewish perspective of salvation history (see Maimonides' *Hilkhoth Melakhim,* chapter 11). Maimonides taught that both Jesus and Muhammed—notice the ecumenical emphasis—were pioneers of the true messianic kingdom, because through the influence of both Jesus and Muhammed the words of the living God, as reflected by our Jewish Torah, have now been spread to the four corners of the earth. Here is the beginning of a Jewish theology of Christianity. Why does the God of Israel have Christianity in His world? Answer: to spread the words of the Torah to the four corners of the earth. Maimonides also taught that, together with the truths of the Torah, the nations have likewise inherited some wrong notions from their ancestors. But these wrong notions will be shed once the true Messiah ultimately appears. What is remarkable is not that a medieval thinker considered his own faith to be "more true" than the faith of others, but that a Jewish contemporary of the Crusades found room for Christians at all within his religious system. Maimonides was somewhat more broad-minded than many Jews today. Maimonides in the twelfth century had a Jewish theology of Christianity, or, at least, he had a starting point for one.

The hint that Maimonides threw out in the twelfth century was taken up by Franz Rosenzweig, one of the greatest Jewish thinkers of the twentieth century. What is remarkable about Franz Rosenzweig is that as a Jew (I emphasize *as a Jew,* because at one point Rosenzweig was on the brink of converting to Christianity, until he rediscovered his own Judaism) he affirmed the truth of John 14:6, "that no man comes to the Father except through Jesus." He was quick, however, to add that the Jews do not have to come to the Father, because they already are with the Father, and have been with the Father ever since Sinai, if not before. In other words, the function of Christianity, according to Franz Rosenzweig, is to bring all other human beings into that relationship with God

Jews already enjoy. Franz Rosenzweig spoke in the imagery of the eternal flame and the eternal rays. Judaism is the eternal flame, the eternal fire; Christianity, the rays. Using a more prosaic metaphor, I think Franz Rosenzweig viewed Christianity as the missionary arm of Judaism. So when Christians sing "Onward, Christian soldiers, marching as to war," they are really our agents.

Rosenzweig says several important things in connection with the role that he assigns to Christianity within his theological scheme. First, the future hopes of Judaism and Christianity are identical. The Jewish hope is represented in Zechariah 14:9, a verse with which every Jewish service concludes: "The Lord will be king over all the earth; on that day the Lord shall be One, and His name One." The Christian hope is revealed in 1 Corinthians 15:24, 28: "Then comes the end, when he delivers the kingdom to God the Father. . . . The Son himself will also be subjected to Him who put all things under him, that God may be everything to every one."

The second observation of Rosenzweig concerns the self-definitions of Jews and Christians. Most Jews are born Jews. There is no particular sacrament that makes a Jew a Jew. Even circumcision, though regarded as an important ritual, is not what makes a Jew, because our girls are not circumcised and they are still Jewish. Certainly, bar mitzvah, or confirmation, is not that which makes a Jew. He is born a Jew, because the covenant that God made with Israel at Mount Sinai was made not only with those "of you who are standing here this day before the Lord our God, but also with those who are not here with us before the Lord our God, even the generations not yet born." That is how God calls the Jews. Outsiders who come in have to submit to certain formalities to be legitimized, legalized in their Jewish status: baptism, circumcision. But the native Jew is born a Jew, because he is born into the covenant God made with Israel. Whereas a Christian is never born a Christian. By Christian definition, a child of Christian parents is born a pagan and becomes a Christian through such things as baptism and, later, confirmation, at which time the baptismal vows are reaffirmed. For Rosenzweig, that is typical of the two ways in which God calls us: the Jew is called into a covenant community; the Christian comes to God through the Christian channel. Both covenants are true: the covenant of Sinai and the covenant of Calvary. Perhaps one is truer than the other, but it is not for us to say which, because only at the eschaton, the final denouement of the historical process, will God let us know who has done the better job of fulfilling God's commandments.

The Rosenzweigian position was echoed from the Christian side by the Reverend James Parkes, an Anglican clergyman born in 1896, who, like Rosenzweig, makes the point that God has made two valid covenants with his children. God has called the faithful community, which is the covenant of Sinai, in which a whole community was called to serve God, and God has called the faithful individual, which is the covenant of Calvary, in which the individual, starting off as a pagan, becomes a worshipper of God through Jesus. Therefore, it is not our business either as Jews or as Christians to steal followers from the other path, because conversionary efforts would only mean that someone is being seduced from the particular station to which God has called him.

Although in my own theology I am pretty much a Rosenzweigian, I can criticize Rosenzweig because he grants Christianity a monopoly. If he affirms that from the non-Jewish world the only other channel to God is Christianity, he does an injustice to Islam and possibly to other religions as well. We in this ecumenical age have become much more conscious of this than Franz Rosenzweig was when he died in 1929. It is not within our human power to place restrictions on God's covenant-making activities. But Rosenzweig was limited by the confines of his own environment, which knew only of Christians and of Jews.

Maimonides was perhaps more ecumenical, because Maimonides found room for the Islamic world, which Rosenzweig did not succeed in doing. However, Rosenzweig marks a great step forward in the development of a Jewish theology of Christianity, first by presenting Christians as more than simply pagans who keep the Laws of the Sons of Noah; he suggests a closer relationship. As a Jew, I find a certain affinity to the Christian, which I do not feel for a Buddhist or a Taoist, however much as a historian of religion I may appreciate the contributions of Buddhism or Taoism.

Second, in Rosenzweig's vision, Christianity is no longer subordinated to Judaism, as it still was for Maimonides. In other words, for Maimonides, Christianity has some truth, but, after all, our own Jewish beliefs are considerably "truer." This attitude disappears for Rosenzweig. Both beliefs are equally true ultimately, though God may or may not tell us which he likes better.

Rosenzweig also defends the covenant of Calvary as a valid covenant with God. And a fourth point he emphasizes is that Jews and Christians, heirs of the same revelation, are part of the same salvation scheme, the same history of salvation. They are not meant to seduce one another from the stations to which they were called by God.

The preceding are the abiding contributions of Franz Rosenzweig toward the creation of a Jewish theology of Christianity. We today have our task of refining those definitions. Theologians amuse themselves by arguing: Are there two valid covenants: Sinai, Calvary? Are we really partners in the same *one* covenant with Christians through Jesus becoming a real part of Israel?

It would be fair to say that the Jews as yet are having an easier time with the first concept—that of *two* valid covenants. Memory of past persecutions is still too fresh to permit the giving of an affirmative answer to the second question: Are we after all, and in spite of the nasty family quarrels we have had, all recipients of the same divine revelation? It is perhaps too early for the bulk of Jewry to assent to that second alternative. I happen to believe that such an assent may ultimately be given. I do not think, I shall be alive at that time. But I would also say that whether an affirmative answer will be given depends at the moment more upon Christians and their relations with Jews than upon Jews. For, as I have tried to point out, Jews do believe "By their fruits ye shall know them."

# The Greek Bible:
# Hidden Treasure for Jews and Christians

MORE THAN SIXTY YEARS ago H. St. J. Thackeray (1923, 9) began his
Schweich Lectures by saying: "The Septuagint has many claims on our
attention. By diffusing for the first time a knowledge of the Hebrew
Scriptures to the world at large it was a *Praeparatio Evangelica* paving
the way for Christianity; it was the Bible of the early Church and the
parent of numerous daughter versions." Here, in a few words, are described the essential merits of the Greek Bible considered from a Christian point of view. It must be added, in the present context, that the Septuagint and its history have had the value of a check on the quality of
Jewish-Christian relations down the centuries and that they are also of
great interest in the ecumenical context of relations between the different Christian confessions.

The previous statement is intended to be a plea of sorts, not directly
for the ideas advanced here but for a renewed interest in the Bible's most
ancient version. Interest in this version has indeed received a great stimulus from recent discoveries such as that of the Dead Sea Scrolls. But we are
still far from having dedicated to the Greek Bible anything like the enormous attention that has been lavished on its Hebrew counterpart.

The most important aspects of present research in the field of Septuagintal studies will be outlined here along with some remarks which

for the specialist will be elementary but which will help to orientate our reflections. But first of all, it is perhaps not superfluous to recall what the Septuagint is exactly.

The term *Septuagint* (LXX) signifies seventy in Latin. It alludes to the legend recounted in the Letter of Aristeas according to which seventy-two elders were sent from Jerusalem to Alexandria in Egypt by the high priest Eleazar at the request of King Ptolemy Philadelphus (285–246 B.C.) to translate into Greek the Torah of Moses (Pentateuch) in order to complete his library. The work of translation was finished in seventy-two days (307). Very soon the figure of seventy-two was rounded off to seventy, and the Septuagint ended up including also the translation of the prophetic and hagiographic portions of the Hebrew Bible accomplished in the following two centuries. When the translator of Sirach wrote his prologue (c. 120 B.C.), the bulk of the Old Testament was already circulating in Greek.

Amidst the legendary details of the account of Aristeas, historians isolate at least one fact, namely, that toward the middle of the third century B.C., in Alexandria, a version of the Torah in Greek appeared; this fact is confirmed by papyrus fragments of about the year 150 B.C. Strictly speaking, the term *Septuagint* denotes this first attempt at a version of the Pentateuch. But the name was quickly extended (in the second century A.D.) to include the translation of the other biblical books, and even to books not accepted in the Hebrew Canon (like Sirach, Tobit), including also those works that are not translations of original Semitic texts (like the book of Wisdom).

Why translate the Torah into Greek? Some authors feel that the translation was done first of all in response to the needs of the synagogue cult. Since the people no longer understood Hebrew, it was necessary, for the needs of the Jewish community, to make a translation: a liturgical motive, therefore, to which some add apologetic aims. Others reject entirely the account of Aristeas (cf. Barthélemy 1974, 23–41). Its historical background corresponds well to the political reality of the time. Moreover the essential point of the tradition on the origins of the LXX is independent of the work of Aristeas. Aristobulus (c. 150 B.C.), for example, knew the tradition of a version made on the initiative of Ptolemy Philadelphus.

The Jewish colony of Alexandria was an important one and, since the

Persian era (cf. Ezra 7), had benefited from privileges that permitted it to live "according to its ancestral laws," that is, according to the Torah. Documents from the first half of the second century attest that the Jews of Alexandria constituted a *politeuma* (corporate body of citizens) which was semiautonomous: the implication is that an Egyptian king had previously conceded to them the right to live according to their own laws. This was, in fact, the work of Ptolemy Philadelphus. But the law was written in Hebrew, which was not the official language of Egypt, hence the king's official measure and the intervention of the high priest in nominating a commission of translators (the number seventy-two, six per tribe, is an obvious embellishment). The LXX, therefore, originated above all from motives of public law (which perhaps accounts for the number of juridical details added to the Hebrew text). It is as a constitution (*nomos* should perhaps be rendered thus) of the *politeuma* of the Jews that the Law of Moses interested the Lagides. The Torah became the fundamental law for all the Jewish communities, for their internal life as well as for their relations with non-Jews and with the authorities, duly recognized by the State and authenticated by the Jewish people (this is the sense of Aristeas [308]).

Probably, this carefully done official version was quickly adopted for liturgical purposes, replacing the fragmentary Targums which could have been in use previously. This liturgical *Sitz im Leben* explains the much less literal character of the books translated after the Torah, whose version served as a lexicon for later translators. The Greek Torah constituted, therefore, the Holy Scriptures of the Jews of the Diaspora and, in Egypt, the legal corpus upon which a whole jurisprudence was constructed, even in the cases in which its text differed from the Hebrew. This may have lasted a hundred years and in this time the prestige of the Alexandrian version did nothing but grow.

However, the criticisms of the Palestinian scribes, which highlighted the differences between the Hebrew Bible and its Greek offspring, gave rise to attempts at revision and recension on the basis of the Hebrew text. The Letter of Aristeas (c. 125 B.C.) was composed in order to establish once and for all the authenticity of the official text. The letter gives an account of all the measures that were taken to ensure an original Hebrew text of exceptional quality (30, 31, 176), including competent translators and ideal conditions of work (301–307). It recalls the ceremony of promulgation in the presence of the whole enthusiastic community (308–309), the guarantees given by the ancients (301), and the curses against anyone who might dare touch that text (311; cf. Deut. 4:2; Deut. 13:1; Rev. 22:18–19).

D. Barthélemy has shown that the letter of Pseudo-Aristeas produced the desired effect (the rabbis would have their revenge 350 years later!): traces of recensions of the Greek version are no longer to be found in the Bible of Philo nor in the later textual tradition of recensions made in the second century B.C. But the forgery could have been successful only if the basic belief which it defended had already been accepted by the Jews as a whole. The famous annual feast on the island of Pharos (where the LXX saw the light of day) served as a springboard for the pamphlet of Aristeas and not vice-versa. The Letter of Aristeas was written to defend the sacred character of a text which was already venerated. The legend may have contributed to its accentuation, but it did not give rise to it. In underlining the divine origin of the Greek translation by allusions to the giving of the Revelation to Moses, the author intends to convey the thought that it has been revealed in the same way (cf. 309 and Exod. 24:3 and 7). It is to the pilgrimage and the "blarney" of the guides that the legend owes its later miraculous details: for example, the detail that each of the translators was closed in a separate room to translate *all* the Torah, with God's inspiration ensuring that all the versions were rigorously similar! (Cohortatio ad Graecos 13; Megillah 9a). Such a story was to lead, in the case of Philo of Alexandria, for example, to the explicit mention of the inspiration of the Septuagint (De vita Mosis II, 37, trans. F. H. Colson). "They became, as it were possessed, and, under inspiration, wrote, not each several scribe something different, but the same word for word, as though dictated to each by an invisible prompter."

The fabulous account of the origin of the LXX was later on to have the negative effect of discrediting the Greek version. The accentuation of its inspired character led to a lessening of the esteem in which it was held and gave rise to an antipathy that impeded its unprejudiced evaluation.

Still, it was an event of considerable importance and a unique experience in antiquity: for the first time, the contents of the sacred books of a religion were accessible to the noninitiated. The Babylonians did not translate their sacred hymns and rites and even in Egypt, though the liturgy of Hellenized Gods like Isis was celebrated in Greek, the authentic sacred books of the Egyptians that the priests carried in procession remained inaccessible to the Greeks. This openness was to preserve the vitality of the biblical Revelation and its power of expansion. It was to impregnate the soul of the proselytes, exactly as it would that of the descendants of Abraham. E. J. Bickerman (1949, 103) remarked in this regard, "The Jews became 'people of the Book' when this Book was rendered into Greek."

It is now necessary to recall some of the stages of the tormented history of a text born under such favorable omens. The testimony of the Letter of Aristeas (311), of Philo and Josephus, not to speak of the New Testament, ensures that the LXX was received with enthusiasm and held in high esteem by the Greek-speaking Jews who considered it their Bible, in the same way the Palestinians regarded their Hebrew Bible. Philo could be considered their spokesman as he explains that the pilgrims, Jews and others, come to Pharos once a year "to do honour to the place in which the *light of that version* first shone out, and also to thank God for the good gift so old yet ever young" (*ibid.*, II, 41).

But the Jewish attitude toward the LXX was heavily influenced by the vicissitudes of history. The turning point is marked by the wars against Rome of 70 and 135 A.D. and by the expansion of Christianity that came forth from Judaism. The Greek-speaking Christians of Jewish origin, like the proselytes, had brought with them their Bible, and they used it henceforth in a polemical fashion in favor of Jesus of Nazareth. This change of attitude took place early on (cf. Justin Martyr, *Dialogue with Trypho* 68.71) and was progressive.

At the beginning of the second century one finds a deliberate attempt to supplant the textual form of the LXX by the version, literal to the extreme, of Aquila (c. 125 A.D.), whose work was greatly praised by the masters R. Eliezer and R. Joshua (J Megillah I, 11, 71 c). The word *Christos* (translating *māshîaḥ*) was replaced by *ēleimmenos* (anointed) and, in Isaiah 7:14 ("The *ʿalmāh* shall be with child" [cf. Matt. 1:23]), the word *parthenos* (virgin) of the LXX was replaced by *neānis* which is closer to the Hebrew *ʿalmāh* (young, unmarried woman).

At this stage, officially it could be said, the Septuagint was abandoned to the Christians. Thus, for Judaism, that audacious experience of openness to the world that had begun 350 years earlier came to an end and the rich literature in the Greek language that blossomed from the experience would henceforth produce nothing more. It is revelatory of the quality of the relations which from now on would exist between Synagogue and Church that what little is known of these texts (apart from Philo and Josephus) is due to Clement of Alexandria and to the Praeparatio Evangelica (Book IX) of Eusebius of Caesarea.

The negative, indeed hostile, attitude of the rabbis in relation to the LXX is final. That which Philo considered as the apparition of a great light was now presented as the coming of darkness on the world (gloss in Megillat Ta'anith) and the tractate Sopherim (I, 7) maintains that the day on which the Greek translation was made "was as hard for Israel as the day the golden calf was made, since the Torah could not be accurately translated."

One dreams of what might have been! For it should not be imagined that the Church inherited ' e LXX as a *res nullius,* abandoned on the field of battle. At its origin there was no intention of separating from Israel in this respect: the first Christians received as the Old Testament a Bible translated into, or interpreted in, Greek, which was considered by the Diaspora Jews as the inspired Bible and used by them as the Palestinians used the original Hebrew text. H. M. Orlinsky (1975) comments: "Had Christianity developed such that it continued to remain within the Jewish fold, the Septuagint would have continued as *the* Bible for those Jewries in the Diaspora (parallel to the Targum and the Hebrew original for the others) for whom Greek was the mother tongue." It is a great pity that the prestige of the LXX was damaged and lacerated by all this wrangling and that its later history reflected the countereffects of that long period in which it was a bone of contention between the Church and Israel.

In the West, the Greek Bible experienced a progressive decline, one which only in recent years has been arrested. Its changing fortunes up to the present day can only be briefly sketched here. Preeminent in this decline was the work of Jerome, "nouveau riche of the Hebrew culture, coated with a rabbinic veneer" (Barthélemy 1974), who, in imposing a return to the pure *veritas hebraica,* succeeded in replacing that which had been the Old Testament of the Church by the Bible of the rabbis. It is striking to discover how little known the LXX was in the West up to the Renaissance and, moreover, to see it become in later times mainly a subject of controversy, as in the seventeenth century between Isaak Vossius and Humphrey Hody (Frankel 1841, 260–66).

The return to the *veritas hebraica* led unfortunately to the LXX being considered as a translation in the strict and modern sense of the word, and the critics enjoyed repeating that the Alexandrian translator "read incorrectly," or "did not understand," paraphrased, and so on. In a word, the impression was created that the Septuagint simply represented a bad and unfaithful translation, composed in an abominable Greek (Wilamowitz). In a number of studies on the LXX, one senses how the various authors have difficulty in keeping an attitude if not sympathetic, at least impartial. The classic Polyglots contributed to making it known; but the typographic disposition itself of the works confirmed the idea that it was merely a version like others such as the Targum, the Syriac Peshitta, and the Latin Vulgate.

The following two facts, eloquent in themselves, show that despite the great work accomplished, there still remains a great deal to do. Even today we still use the *Lexicon in LXX* of Johann Friedrich Schleussner (1820–1829), and there exists no project to compile another (Aland 1977, 42). On the other hand, only two volumes of the Pentateuch (Genesis and Deuteronomy) have appeared in the Göttingen critical edition.

Fortunately, thanks to parallel researches on the Targum and Midrash, it is becoming clearer that the Bible in Greek is a very different thing from a simple translation and that it represents perhaps a hidden treasure. That brings to mind the recent story of a former French soldier in Tahiti to whom a native friend gave a picture as a souvenir on his departure. On returning to France he hung it in the kitchen where it remained until one day a visitor who happened to be a connoisseur discovered that it was a gorgeous Gauguin. One may well ask how the specialists of the Bible managed to overlook for so long the riches at hand in their Septuagint. It may be useful, therefore, to offer some reflections on the importance of this treasure.

E. Nestle, in his article "Septuagint" in the *Dictionary of the Bible* (IV, 437) recalls that Ferd. Hitzig of Heidelberg began his course of exegesis on the Old Testament in the following manner: "Gentlemen, have you a Septuagint? If not, sell whatever you have, and buy a Septuagint."

Several classical arguments exist for the Septuagint, such as its importance for the vocabulary and the content of the New Testament, for the Christian mission, for patristic theology, and so on. I will restrict myself to recalling certain facts.

The date itself of the Greek version lends it great importance. It is the only version definitely anterior to the fixing of the biblical canon and going back therefore to a time in which the Bible was still in its formative stage. In addition, since it provides a literal word for word version of the Torah, it represents the most ancient authoritative witness of the Hebrew text of the Pentateuch, thus permitting a control of the traditional text. Since it was produced by competent Palestinian scholars, *au fait* with the common interpretation, it can equally well be used to restore the lost sense of Hebrew passages which are obscure, corrupted, or deliberately altered for theological or legalistic reasons.

Since the Qumran discoveries we know that there existed a plurality of textual traditions and that the LXX is based on a non-Masoretic type of Hebrew text related to the textual tradition found in Qumran. It is now established that the Greek versions of Jeremiah and Job, whose translators have been often accused of adding, suppressing, displacing, and so on, represent a non-Masoretic type of text. Furthermore, D. Barthélemy (1963) has proved that the remains of a Greek scroll of the Minor Prophets (from Naḥal Hever) contains a systematic first century (c. 30–50 A.D.) revision of the Septuagint's original rendering. This shows that for the Palestinian Jews the value of the Greek version as Revelation resided in its substantial agreement with the original Hebrew, and also that attempts at revision were anterior to the Judeo-Christian polemics.

The importance of the LXX has been realized more since it began to be considered in itself, as having its own personality (and not only as a more or less faithful reflection of the original Hebrew), and since its nature has been better defined. S. Jellicoe (1968, 342) writes, "So common is the tacit assumption that the LXX is but a handmaid to the study of the Hebrew text of the Old Testament and the grammar and vocabulary of the New that it has failed to secure its just due as a body of literature *in its own right*." One finds such judgments coming more and more frequently from the pens of specialists of the LXX.

The Greek Bible has been used too exclusively for textual criticism. It has indeed an important role to play in this area and the agreements of the LXX and the Temple Scroll of Qumran against the Masoretic text have provided further proof. But this should not be its only use. Moreover, the nonrecognition of the true nature of the ancient versions (whose "variants" often do not in any way imply a different *Vorlage*) has caused critics to commit not a few blunders. It is noticeable that the *Biblia Hebraica Stuttgartensia* is much more reserved in its use of the versions than the *Biblia Hebraica* of R. Kittel. To regard the LXX as a version like the others and simply as a witness to the ancient state of the Hebrew text is to overlook its origin and to pay little attention to its particular point of view and to its individuality. It must be considered rather as constituting a whole that is in reality an original creation. S. Jellicoe concluded, "As a literature alone its influence was enormous, and the recognition of the Greek Old Testament as an independent, rather than ancillary, field of study has in turn an important bearing on methodology." In particular, the content of the LXX must be judged on its own merits and no longer solely in its relationship (more or less faithful) to the Masoretic text. That is what I intend when I use the term *personality*.

The Septuagint was made in a tradition, and it could not be a pure reproduction of the Hebrew. When the translators began to tackle the huge enterprise, half of the work had already been done. They knew the biblical text intimately and were fully acquainted with its interpretation in the lively community of which they were a part. It is that exegesis which they expressed in Greek. The deviations from the original text are not to be explained as mostly due to the personal initiative of a translator but to the life itself of the Word of God in the faith of the people. And this is what ensures that it is the authentic message of Revelation that is transmitted, under a new form. Victor Tcherikover (1957, 42) noted: "It is obvious that for Aristeas, and for Jews like him, it was not merely a translation, but, in some sense, a second creation of the Bible. And we can guess the reason. . . . It was not only the Bible in Greek, it was a Greek Bible in its thought and expression." It contains certain accentuations which reveal definite preoccupations, with an insistence more or less strong on particular aspects of the biblical message (for example, the stronger wisdom component, the exaltation of the Torah, and so on). That the LXX has its own personality is an unavoidable conclusion. It suffices to recall the new or completely transformed texts (like the Greek Esther, translated in Jerusalem [cf. Brownlee 1966]) which it contains, in order to make this point. Therefore, one can legitimately speak of a theology of the Septuagint, as Kittel's TDNT as a whole, as well as innumerable other studies, has already demonstrated. One must of course define more clearly its relationship to that which is called biblical theology.

While the Hebrew text was still in a fluid state and the various Hebrew redactors were working on a noncanonical text, the Greek translators on the contrary had before them, for each book, a unique and complete Hebrew text which was already considered as Holy Writ. The Hebrew text came into being one book after another through a successive accumulation of documents and traditions. The books of the LXX, on the other hand, were created in one concentrated attempt. It is for this reason that H. M. Orlinsky (1975, 108) calls on critics "to approach the Septuagint with the utmost respect, indeed with far greater respect and caution than in dealing with the received (so-called masoretic) Hebrew text" and not to treat it in a cavalier fashion.

The Greek version has, consequently, a fundamental unity (not a homogeneity) which it owes to its origin and to its transmission in a definite milieu (that of Alexandrian Judaism). As for its relative unity of content, one finds here the conceptions of God and man of Diaspora Judaism which are substantially uniform, a conception of the world formed by Revelation in the centuries old encounter of the Greek and Jewish thought. Once completed, it would be accepted as a Bible in its definitive form, with its errors, additions, diversity of documents, exactly as will happen in the case of the Hebrew Bible. In the light of this, one can question whether it is legitimate for a modern translation to do as the Jerusalem Bible did for Numbers 24 (the prophecies of Balaam), namely, to follow sometimes the Hebrew and sometimes the Greek. Is this not a case of creating a new Bible from the spare parts of two others?

As I have pointed out, the particular personality of the LXX becomes apparent only when one realizes that it is not a translation in the modern sense, but a version of a sacred book as it was then understood, namely, the faithful transmission of the *content* of the message as it was then perceived and lived in the Hellenistic-Jewish communities. That is to say, it is the text with its interpretation.

If the translation of the Torah is fairly literal by reason of its preeminence in the hierarchy of the biblical books, the same cannot be said for the other sections. The traditional interpretation that was current in the synagogue and in the school was woven into the fabric of the version itself. It was this tendency to absorb all the explanations that rendered the text, as G. Vermes (1975, 137) says apropos of the Targum of Onkelos, "intelligible and theologically acceptable."

The text is transmitted, therefore, in such a way that it is adapted and actualized in order to bring it to life. You will recognize in this the essential aspect of the midrashic activity (already present in the Bible) which considers Scripture as a living Word, and not as a mummy (Frankel 1841, 260–66). Today we would say that the Bible is a musical score that must be brought to life by ever new readings. While displaying much greater sobriety, the LXX may be compared to the Aramaic Targum with which it shares all of its preoccupations as well as its exegetical procedures and techniques, aspects which have been abundantly illustrated from Z. Frankel (1851) to L. Prijs (1948).

If every translation already supposes an interpretation and a certain transposition, then one can see all the more how a deliberate midrashic activity would end by conferring on the Greek Bible a singular originality. Its value can no longer be said to reside only in its exact reproduction of the content of the Hebrew text (in which its value as Scripture would be limited, according to some), or in the fixing of a certain number of doctrinal developments barely sketched or suggested in the original, but also in these new elements which the midrash draws from the text itself. It is often such new contributions that must be examined in order to understand the later use which was to be made of these texts (as, for example, in the New Testament).

The midrashic character of the LXX is well recognized by the specialists who frequently speak today of theological exegesis, midrashic renderings, exegetical character/additions/translations, interpretative version, midrashic type exegesis, and so on.

S. Lieberman (1962, 50) has justly characterized the Septuagint as "the oldest of our preserved Midrashim," and M. H. Goshen-Gottstein (1963) speaks of its "exegetical texture, which may be described as midways between the *Peshat* character of the Peshitta and the *Derash* features of the Targum." Z. Frankel and L. Prijs have studied a great number of haggadic and halakic elements (narrative and legal material) which have passed into the LXX and which have exact parallels in later Jewish literature.

The Septuagint may be considered, then, as the result of a process of evolution and growth of the biblical text which has come about through the continuous practice of an exegesis, founded on the authority of the text itself, and which goes beyond it, in view of a constant adaptation to the changing needs of the community. The process which explains the formation of the Old Testament has been active, therefore, in the making of the Greek Bible. D. Barthélemy (1965) sustains that "the OT matured in Alexandria," attaining there its final form willed by God, to which the message of the New Testament would be directly linked. It was at the level of the testimony of its Greek version, rather than the Hebrew original, that the Christians found in the Bible the outline of the mystery of Christ. But this is a ticklish subject which cannot be dealt with here. We must content ourselves with pointing out some examples of what that actualization brought to the text, from concrete facts on the historical level to the more important theological conceptions.

Certain changes represent intentional adaptations to an Egyptian milieu, as E. Bickerman (1976, 200–24) has shown for certain legal interpretations and for the use of technical terms related to the administration (*diadochos*) and the cult (*pastophorion*). One detail in Exodus 10:13 may be well situated in Egypt: the east wind which brings up the locusts is changed into a south wind (*notos*), because in Egypt the locusts come from Nubia or, to give it its modern name, Sudan.

The rabbinic tradition itself admits that the translators occasionally modified the text out of deference to pagan sensitivity, and it preserved a list of passages "changed . . . for King Ptolemy" (Mekhilta Exod. 14; Megillah 9a). But without modification of the original text, the rendering of Exodus 22:27 is remarkable: "You shall not revile the *gods*" (in Hebrew, Elohim means God). This could be interpreted as an attitude of tolerance, and V. Tcherikover (1957, 42) notes that the Jews who only read Greek "sincerely believed in Moses' tolerant attitude towards the heathen gods." The emperor Julian (Contra Galilaeos 238c) would use that text to defend respect for the gods and polytheism, and Philo, like Josephus, interpreted it literally.

The classic example of historical actualization is provided by Isaiah 9:11 where the LXX (c. 150 B.C.) replaces the enemies of Israel, "Aram on the east and the Philistines on the west," with "Syria . . . and the Greeks." M. Hengel sees here "a reference . . . to the successes of the Parthians against the Seleucids and the annihilation of Macedonia by the Romans" during the second century B.C.

D. W. Gooding (1964, 1965, 1967, 1969) has shown how entire historical books (like both 1 Kings and 2 Kings) have been retouched in order to adapt them to the evolved ideas concerning certain protagonists like Solomon, Achab, or Jeroboam. Apropos of this, it should be carefully noted that the image of personages of the Bible (Abraham, Moses, Job), the interpretation of certain episodes (the sacrifice of Isaac, the covenant of Sinai), the theological significance of Jewish feasts, and so on, can be quite different from that which the Hebrew Bible presents. For New Testament exegesis it is obviously essential to know what the interpretation of a given biblical text looked like in contemporary hermeneutics.

For example, the Hebrew text of Jeremiah 31:8 may be translated, "I will gather them from the ends of the world, with the *blind and the lame* in their midst" (italics added). The Greek translator, however, offers a completely different text: "I shall gather them . . . *in the feast of the Passover*" (italics added). The interpretation is certainly intentional since the Hebrew consonants of "blind and lame" could easily be read "the time of Pesach." A new overtone is thus added to the themes associated with the Passover: the announcement of the great return from exile is directly related to the paschal festival. Whatever be the origin of that interpretation, it is thus that the text of Greek Jeremiah was read in the first century.

It is on the theological level that the contribution of the LXX in the fixing of the development of the religious conceptions of Israel is most striking. It is on this level too that it reveals itself as indispensable in the explanation of how Christian theology could have developed from Judaism. Here I am able to offer only a few allusions to that which touches the conception of God, the messianic expectation, and the ideas concerning eschatology, future life, and Resurrection.

The Hebrew Old Testament already showed a tendency to underline more and more the divine transcendence, and certain interpretations of the LXX carry this process further. Scholars are divided in their interpretation of how the translators treated the anthropomorphisms (attribution to God of human characteristics). H. M. Orlinsky (1975, 107) states that "it would hardly have occurred to any Jew to think of God anthropomorphically" and that the LXX did not avoid them; if it did, "it was not for any theological reason." All that one can affirm is that it is impossible to uncover precise rules and that each translator follows his own method. But once realized, the version lent itself now and then to spiritualizing interpretations. Thus, in the case of Exodus 24:10, "They saw the God of Israel" becomes in Greek, "They saw the place [*topos*] where the God of Israel stood" (cf. 11). In Exodus 15:3 (cf. Isa. 41:13) God is called "The Lord, the Man of war." How can such a thing be said of God? The Greek gives the phrase a quite different meaning: "The Lord crushing wars" (*syntribōn polemous*). The verb *crush* is often linked to the eschatological context of the destruction of the oppressor. God becomes the "crusher of wars," an expression which has a messianic flavor and will become traditional (cf. Jth. 9:7 and 16:2).

The question of messianism covers an immense area full of pitfalls, but it is of utmost importance for the Christian reading of the Old Testament. The simple fact that, in the LXX, Daniel was promoted to the category of the Prophets and that the term *māshiaḥ* is always translated by *Christos* is probably not without relevance.

A study of this point should involve the whole LXX, for the messianic idea can appear in a single term—like the demonstrative masculine *autos* used after the neuter *sperma* in Genesis 3:15 or even the *parthenos* of Isaiah 7:14—or equally in the reinterpretation of whole chapters—like Isaiah 14, which is characterized in the LXX by a strong messianic accent.

Apropos of the prophecies of Balaam in Numbers 24, Z. Frankel (1851, 182) has explained how the particular situation of the Jews in Egypt led to the messianic theme being much more explicit in the Greek version. Thus Numbers 24:17 reads: "A star shall rise out of Jacob, a man [*anthrôpos,* instead of the obscure *shēbet*] shall spring out of Israel." The Hebrew of verse 7 is also very obscure; it speaks literally about "dripping water from buckets." But everything is clear in the Greek: "There shall come a man [*anthrôpos*] out of his seed, and he shall rule over many nations. His kingdom shall be exalted above *Gog* [in Hebrew, *Agag*] and his kingdom shall be increased." Note that Gog reappears in verse 23 (correct *Og* of the text), thus adding an eschatological tone (cf. Ezra 38–39) and recalling the association of Gog and the Messiah which will become traditional (Targum Num. 11:26; Rev. 20). The interpretation of all the chapter is therefore quite coherent.

The presence of a strong messianic preoccupation characterizes certain translators (for example, that of Isaiah) and one can glean from the LXX many details related to this particular topic (cf. Ps. 2). It is not surprising that Christian writers found in such reelaborated biblical material a rich source for their apologetics.

In regard to eschatology, one notes a particular interest of certain translators in personal eschatology and in the afterlife. The use made of the term *zoē* (life) shows that this concept often involves the blessings of salvation and of future life. The translator of Job used a *Vorlage* similar to the one behind our Masoretic text; but, as D. H. Gard (1954) affirms, "in regard to the concept of the future life in the book of Job M [HT] and G[reek] differ significantly. In M [cf. 14:14] only a question concerning the possibility of a future life is raised. In G the future life is stated as a fact" (cf. also 42:17). This corresponds to a recent acquisition of biblical theology (Dan. 12:2; Isa. 26:19), and it is clearly expressed also in other witnesses of Hellenistic Judaism (2 Macc. 7 [cf. Nickelsburg 1972]).

By replacing the phrase "As the days of a tree, so the days of my people" of Isaiah 65:22 with "As the days of the tree of life . . .", the Greek version establishes the doctrinal progress which had been made by the second century B.C. in substituting the promise of an extraordinary longevity (that of the trees) with that of immortality. A comparison between the Hebrew text and the Greek version of Sirach reveals the same progress in the affirmation of eschatological beliefs which are assured from now on (survival and retribution in the afterlife, resurrection: 7:17; 48:11).

After what we have seen, it is not difficult to perceive why the Septuagint has recovered a place that it should never have lost in the consideration of theologians and exegetes. As a conclusion I would like to propose for your reflection various aspects of that revalorization.

First, the textual criticism of the Old Testament remains more than ever largely dependent on Septuagintal studies. But one notes a more prudent use of this version, and its interpretative nature is better recognized. We know also, since the discoveries of Qumran, that the Masoretic Bible was not *the* Bible of the Palestinians in the first century and that the latter was often close to the textual form preserved in the LXX (cf. Cross 1961, 168–94).

Second, in a significant way, the Alexandrian Bible illustrates the approach of the ancients to the sacred text. The attitudes of the Greek translators is no different from that of the scribes toward the Hebrew Bible which, as G. von Rad has shown in his *Theology of the OT,* is a compilation of texts, read and reread, adapted and rewritten in a form which is never a simple reproduction of the previous stage of the text.

Third, the LXX, which was the Bible of the Jews before it became the Christian Bible, is being considered more as an important witness of the ancient Jewish tradition and of the interpretation of Scripture at a crucial point in the development of the two religious traditions. In addition, it gives us information on the Jewish religion of the Diaspora, and its study must be conducted parallel to that of the so-called intertestamental literature in which is expressed that evolved form of biblical religion that is called Judaism. In seeking to discover the intentions (more or less conscious) of the Greek translators (not those attributed to them by later Jewish and Christian users!), it will emerge that they are above all witnesses of the faith of their time and of Hellenistic Judaism.

Fourth, from a different perspective, the LXX offers an introduction to later Jewish writings: this is because it is situated at the beginning of a straight line that leads to rabbinic literature. Mention has already been made of its affinities with Midrash. Many of its passages can only be understood in the light of later midrashic interpretations: an inexplicable aspect this, if one does persist in putting it into the category of a translation.

Fifth, here the relationship Scripture-Tradition can be studied "from life." I cannot expand on this, and a remark must suffice: the faith of the Old Testament was transmitted not only by a text, but also by a tradition of which a part, it must be presumed, passed in turn into the Greek version, providing a striking example of the impact of Tradition on Scripture.

And sixth, the history itself of the LXX and the role it had played forces one to acknowledge its privileged place in Revelation. It was through this version that the Diaspora Jews (even Philo himself) came to know the Word of God, while their Palestinian coreligionists had the Hebrew text and the Targum. The New Testament itself uses it without worrying about its deviations from the original. Indeed, it sometimes founded important arguments on such modifications (like the resurrection of Jesus in Acts 2:27 or the mission to the pagans in Acts 15: 16–17). The Greek version had been simply assimilated to the original. It was much more than an Authorized Version.

In considering the importance of its role, some Catholic exegetes (Benoit 1961, 3–12; Auvray 1952; Grelot 1964) have been led to pose anew the problem of the Septuagint's inspiration, a question which Frankel (1841) had already considered *Unsinn* (a nonsense) and definitely resolved in the negative. They have called on theologians to examine more thoroughly the notion of inspiration and to develop it, in order to give an answer to the many pressing questions posed by the Greek text. The means taken by God to reveal himself seem to have been more flexible and varied than is suggested by those listed in the manuals of classic theology. But this brings us into another area of discussion which is not my concern here. Whatever the case may be, the unique place of the Septuagint in the history of the people of God, Jewish and Christian, implies a special intervention of Divine Providence, which one would like to see more clearly defined. The present-day interest in the problems connected with authority, canon, and inspiration should contribute to this clarification (see Ackroyd 1977; Sanders 1972).

## Literature Cited

Ackroyd, Peter R. "Original Text and Canonical Text." *Union Seminary Quarterly Review* 32 (1977): 166–73.

Aland, Barbara. *Bericht der Stiftung zur Forderung der neutestamentlichen Textforschung.* Münster, 1977.

Auvray, P. "Comment se pose le problème de l'inspiration de la Septante?" *Revue biblique* 59 (1952): 321–36.

Barthélemy, D. *Les devanciers d'Aquila.* Supplement to V.T. X. Leiden, 1963.

———. "L'Ancien Testament a mûri à Alexandrie." *Theol. Zeitschrift* 21 (1965): 358–70.

————. "Pourquoi la Torah a-t-elle été traduite en grec?" In *On Language, Culture and Religion,* edited by Matthew Blach. La Hague-Paris, 1974.

Benoit, P. *Exégèse et Théologie.* Vol. 1. Paris, 1961.

Bickerman, E. J. "The Historical Foundations of Postbiblical Judaism." In *The Jews,* edited by L. Finkelstein. Vol. 1. New York, 1949.

————. *Studies in Jewish and Christian History.* Pt. 1. Leiden, 1976.

Brownlee, W. H. "Le livre d'Esther et la royauté divine." *Revue biblique* 73 (1966): 161–85.

Cross, Frank Moore. *The Ancient Library of Qumrân and Modern Biblical Studies.* Rev. ed. New York, 1961.

Frankel, Z. *Vorstudien in der Septuaginta.* Leipzig, 1841.

————. *Ueber den Einfluss der palästinischen Exegese auf die alexandrinische Hermeneutik.* Leipzig, 1851.

Gard, D. H. "The Concept of Future Life according to the Greek Translator of the Book of Job." *JBL* 73 (1954): 143.

Gooding, D. W. *ZAW* 35 (1964): 269–80.

————. "Pedantic Timetabling in 3rd Book of Reigns." *Vetus Testamentum* 15 (1965): 153–66.

————. "The Septuagint's Rival Versions of Jeroboam's Rise to Power." *Vetus Testamentum* 17 (1967): 173–89.

————. *Textus* 7 (1969): 1–29.

Goshen-Gottstein, M. H. "Theory and Practice of Textual Criticism." *Textus* 3 (1963): 130.

Grelot, P. "Sur l'inspiration et la canonicité de la Septante." *Sciences ecclesiastiques* 15 (1964): 387–418.

Jellicoe, S. *The Septuagint and Modern Study.* Oxford, 1968.

Lieberman, S. *Hellenism in Jewish Palestine.* New York, 1962.

Nickelsburg, George W. E. *Resurrection, Immortality, and Eternal Life in Intertestamental Judaism.* Harvard Theological Studies, vol. 26. Cambridge, Mass., 1972.

Orlinsky, H. M. "The Septuagint as Holy Writ and the Philosophy of the Translators." *Hebrew Union College Annual* 46 (1975): 103.

Prijs, L. *Jüdische Tradition in der Septuaginta.* Leiden, 1948.

Sanders, James A. "Adaptable for Life: The Nature and Function of Canon." In *Magnalia Dei, The Mighty Acts of God,* edited by Frank M. Cross, 531–60. New York, 1976.

————. *Torah and Canon.* Philadelphia, 1972.

Tcherikover, Victor. *Corpus Papyrorum Judaicarum.* Vol. 1. Cambridge, Mass., 1957.

Thackeray, H. St. J. Schweich Lectures. In *The Septuagint and Jewish Worship*. 2d ed. London, 1923.

Vermes, G. *Post-Biblical Jewish Studies*. Leiden, 1975.

# Jewish Tradition and New Testament Interpretation

ROGER LEDÉAUT

EVERYONE KNOWS THAT Christianity springs from Judaism. But when it comes to drawing practical conclusions from that fact, we are far from agreeing on the depth and the extent of its deep-rootedness. However, the fact itself should never be overlooked in any study of Christian origins. One aspect of the vast problem of studying Christianity through Judaism can be formulated in this way: Christian exegesis must always take into account the early Jewish Tradition which constitutes the real intermediary between the Old Testament and the New Testament. That sounds like a truism. And yet, neotestamentary studies often start directly from biblical data, omitting the essential link of contemporary Jewish conceptions, so that we are faced with the question of method. By Jewish Tradition I mean traditional interpretation of Scripture at the time of Jesus, leaving aside certain aspects (like Tradition as such, the role of oral Law) which, however, touch closely the questions we are going to deal with.

First, what are the sources at our command? Obviously all the texts of the intertestamental period are important witnesses to the early exegetical tradition; above all, the so-called Dead Sea Scrolls (particularly the scriptural commentaries), the Apocrypha (especially those which rewrite biblical history in their own way, such as the Book of Jubilees, the

Biblical Antiquities of Pseudo-Philo), and even the Jewish Antiquities of Josephus. Apocalyptic writings for which the New Testament manifests some regard (Jude, vv. 9 and 14) are essential for the reconstruction of the New Testament background. As a matter of fact, these Jewish writings were preserved by Christians, whereas they were left out by rabbinic orthodoxy.

In a study of intertestamental writings, the less-known compositions, especially the ancient biblical versions, are equally important, however. The reasons for their importance are too numerous to discuss here, but a few will suffice. First, even when interpreted according to the different Jewish trends, with varying perspectives and methods, the Bible is still the common meeting ground for the whole of first-century Judaism. The Torah, especially after Ezra, had for centuries been the foundation of the religion of Israel. The biblical translations were the first link between the Bible and its traditional interpretation. It was on them that Jews relied for their understanding of the sacred text. The Aramaic version (Targum) in particular has often been called the Bible of the Jewish populace (Harris 1920–21).

Second, targumic literature is probably the best source for understanding the religious ideas common to the whole of Judaism, as opposed to the "orientated" interpretations of sectarian movements (like Qumran and Christianity). It is also somewhat less censured than rabbinic writings. Being essentially liturgical (and not educational like the Midrashim), it witnesses to an average, popular, and universal level of religious culture—that of the mainstream of Judaism, which gave Christianity its first adherents. In fact, the Bible was translated according to the generally accepted meaning, whereas it can be supposed that such works as the Apocrypha and the Dead Sea Scrolls reached only a certain stratum of the Jewish world. The Targum tells us how the Old Testament was generally understood.

And third, these statements will have raised some questions—in particular, that of the dating of the targumic texts. The discovery of Targums at Qumran and many recent studies prove the early date of written Targumim and the antiquity of the traditions they have preserved. Moreover, as it is a question of exegetical traditions, even more recent Jewish literature has something to say about it: these traditions, under different textual forms, were transmitted with remarkable fidelity to the content. (Some traditions extant only in late midrashim can be found in Josephus [cf. Daube 1956, 190].) We can also draw the same conclusions from the Septuagint alone, which provides unquestionably old texts to illustrate the statements that follow.

*Jewish exegetical tradition reveals the ancient approach to Scripture.* This attitude toward the sacred text was to be that of the authors of the New Testament, that of Jesus himself. The problem of the use of the Old Testament in the New Testament must be situated in this wider perspective.

The Bible was considered a sacred book (in its Hebrew form as in the Greek), but not as a mummy (Z. Frankel). The Old Testament itself reveals a living, not a mechanical, transmission. The scribes and, above all, the early interpreters considered it perfectly legitimate to add to or to remove from the text, expound or even modify the meaning to adapt it to new facts. "The authors of P [Priestly Code] did not hesitate to rewrite [their] sources entirely removing whatever conflicted with their theories and adding whatever was needed to integrate their work" (Pfeiffer 1948, 206). Adaptation of the Hebrew text is seen also in the development of its ancient recensions before it was fixed in the so-called Masoretic text, as F. M. Cross has shown, just as in the history of the Samaritan Pentateuch (Cross 1964; Purvis 1968). Changes in the text are not to be categorized as arbitrary, nor set down to inaccuracies on the part of the scribes, but were often consciously intended. The liberties which surprise us are due to midrashic tendencies, always to be found in the transmission of Scripture, which requires unceasing adaptation. The book of Chronicles is a kind of Midrash in comparison with its sources in Samuel and Kings; it has even been called Targum. Cannot a similar attitude be recognized in the New Testament, for example in Luke in the material developed there which is not found in Mark or Matthew? What has been termed "the liberties of Luke" (E. Osty) are phenomena similar to "targumism," (i.e., a tendency to elucidate, to enlarge upon, to adapt the biblical text), frequent not only in the versions, but in the Old Testament itself (cf. Mark 5 : 25 – 26 and Luke 8 : 43).

The conceptions found in early Jewish exegesis are indeed very different from ours; thus the understanding of the unity of Scripture, read as it stands without any criticism, allowed the interpreter to appeal to future history as well as to the past. Treating all of Scripture as one unit, he had to reconcile apparent contradictions in it, mainly in the body of laws which belong to different epochs and contexts. The difficulties were overcome by criteria that seem childish to us—for instance, the many meanings that one verse can have.

To discover the meaning, techniques of various kinds were used, some of which at least would be rejected by the modern exegetes but at that time were considered valid (recourse to analogy, new divisions in the text or even in words, homophony, gematria based on the numerical value of the letters, *notariqon*, *'al tiqrey*, which means "do not read so . . . but"). L. Prijs (1948) has discovered that a number of these techniques appear already in the LXX; W. H. Brownlee (1951) and E. Slomovic (1969) have found them in the biblical commentaries of Qumran. Therefore, similar methods must be expected in the New Testament. The key to the Scriptures henceforth is Jesus of Nazareth, the center of history and revelation; but the methods of interpretation could not have been changed overnight. Even the Gospel of John contains traces of rabbinic discussions and midrashic exegesis (John 1 : 51; 3 : 14; 7 : 38). These are the methods that allowed Paul and James to reach different conclusions from the same text of Genesis 15 : 6 ("And [Abraham] believed the Lord; and he reckoned it to him as righteousness"): justification through faith (Gal. 3 : 6) or by works (James 2 : 23 ff). The Targum, the first exegesis of Scripture, provides numerous examples of these procedures.

Parallels to certain Jewish practices can also be found in the New Testament: quoting only part of a text, omitting the point (cf. Matt. 21 : 16); reasoning in terms of a much broader context than the one actually quoted (cf. 2 Cor 3 : 16); omitting the parallel text in an argumentation by analogy or quoting a text in a totally different meaning (2 Cor 4 : 13 and Ps. 116 : 10: "I believed, and so I spoke").

Another fact is important: the incredible capacity for memorizing in early Judaism. S. Lieberman (1962, 52) writes that the rabbis knew their Bible by heart (cf. Gerhardsson 1961). This certainly explains how easy it was to juggle with rapprochements, to find parallel passages, produce quotations which amalgamate several texts. Let us remember the preponderance of oral culture in ancient civilizations. In Judaism, the oral Torah is put on the same footing as the written Torah; and one could quote indifferently saying *shene'emar* ("as it is said") or in Aramaic, *diketib* ("as it is written"). Certain uses of *akouein* ("to hear") in the New Testament recall the rabbinic *shema'tetā*, a tradition received orally. In a discussion (on the relation between Passover and Sabbath) Hillel was unable, after a whole day's dissertation, to make his point of view accepted, until finally he was able to say that "he had heard" from Shemaya and Abtalion (J. Pesahim VI, 1, 33 a). We cannot omit here the "You have heard that it was said" repeated in Matthew 5.

The most interesting contribution from the Qumran writings and targumic literature for an understanding of the New Testament is well formulated in the concluding words of an article by Meir Gertner (1962), entitled "Midrashim in the New Testament." "Clearly parallel sayings or similar conceptions are not so much to be sought as similarity in midrashic techniques and methods and identical ways of scriptural interpretation."

*Scripture is not separated from Tradition, meaning that it was transmitted with its interpretation.* In the Talmud (Kiddushin 49 b) the question is asked: What is Torah? And the answer is: The interpretation of Torah. This supposes that the teaching of Scripture can be conveyed only by means of interpretation (*midrash* in the text); the knowledge of Torah alone is insufficient. Tradition is the life of the text. Josephus is a good witness to that fact. After having stated that he intends neither to add to nor subtract from anything whatever in the biblical text that he claims to retell (Antiquities I, 17), he gives a digest of traditional interpretation, so that S. Rappaport was able to write the book *Agada und Exegese bei Flavius Josephus* (Vienna 1930), showing, among other things, that the author took his inspiration quite often from targumic tradition.

Former translators indeed spontaneously included in their version the meaning accepted in their time and in their milieu. If to translate is necessarily to interpret, it can be said that the work was already half done before they began. They were never faced with a completely fresh text straight from the hands of the author. As the Bible was written then (without vowels), the traditional pronunciation was itself an interpretation! Even the most obscure passages had received a traditional explanation. The Word of God could not be without significance, so it was their very respect for the text that impelled them to explain its meaning. Therefore untranslatable passages are never found in the Targum, any more than suspension points are found in our Bibles. Everything that helps to make a text understandable (cf. Neh. 8 : 8) is included: explanations, glosses, allusions to parallel passages, and so on. We can do no better than to quote T. W. Manson (1945). "We are long accustomed to distinguish carefully between the text, which—in more senses than one—is sacred, and the commentary upon it or the expositions of it. We tend to think of the text as objective fact and interpretation as subjective opinion. It may be doubted whether the early Jewish and Christian translators and expositors of Scripture made any such sharp distinction . . . accurate reproduction of the traditional wording of the divine oracles took second place to publication of what was held to be their essential meaning and immediate application."

Thus, the versions more or less amplified by actualized contemporary exegesis became witnesses to the religious ideas of a definite period. These conceptions have often evolved in what touches such important topics as the concept of God, messianism, eschatology. This process of reinterpretation is already attested to in the Old Testament itself (in the use of former prophets by latter prophets or of earlier documents by later biblical writers). Any biblical text suggested an orchestration of commentaries transmitted by oral tradition, which gradually became crystallized in Targum and Midrash. Reference to a text also meant referring to its current exegesis. All kinds of factors—apologetic, catechetical, polemical—influenced the understanding of the biblical text, and it was felt that by presenting it under an actualized form its true meaning was brought to light.

Scripture should also normally feed *paraenesis* (exhortation) and bring spiritual light and comfort (Rom. 15 : 4). This is how Christians, following along the lines of Jewish homiletics, have continued to present the patriarchs as models, often at the price of some touching up. At Antioch in Pisidia, after the reading of the Torah and the Prophets (Acts 13 : 15), Paul is asked for "a word of exhortation for the people." This is far from a speculative, objective, academic use of Scripture. Scripture, which had inspired the Maccabean resistance (1 Macc. 12 : 9; 2 Macc. 15 : 9), is also presented in the New Testament as "useful for teaching, for reproof, correction, and training in righteousness" (2 Tim. 3:16). A. Geiger (1928, 452) has given a good description of the ancient versions when writing about the Targum: "This translation . . . was not a pure word for word reproduction; it was rather *explanation, development, interpretation,* and *exhortation* adapted to the present situation; therefore, not infrequently, *transformation.*" The insertion of the deuterocanonical books in the LXX, as well as the apparition of rewritten Bibles, such as Jubilees or Biblical Antiquities, show also the creative activity of Tradition side by side with Scripture.

Enrichment of the texts is a fact that no exegete can afford to overlook, especially the constant development under midrashic influence. The New Testament incorporates evolved religious conceptions that were no longer exactly those of the Old Testament. Dealing with ethical subjects in the Apocalyptic, R. H. Charles pointed out that "the ethical teaching on these subjects in apocalyptic is a vast advance on that of the Old Testament, and forms the indispensable link which in this respect connects the Old Testament with the New Testament" (cf. Dentan 1964).

Progressively, *theologoumena* (generally accepted doctrines) were established in Judaism, in the light of which the old texts were understood. But it happened sometimes that these conceptions finally got into the biblical text itself (for instance, the doctrine of merit and retribution, the role of Torah). It was the return impact of Tradition on Scripture; and the New Testament specialist should not forget this Scripture-Tradition dialectic which demonstrates the life of the Word of God within his people.

Tradition itself became a hedge against the fantasy of interpreters (J. Pesahim VI, 1, 33a) who were supposed to utilize the hermeneutic rules not on their own initiative but by tradition. Therefore many interpretations in ancient Jewish literature can be considered not as particular points of view of an individual, but as an echo of a common doctrine. As synagogue liturgy constitutes the link between Scripture and oral tradition, it is obvious how precious it would be to have still the Targum of the Torah and the Prophets in its original, unrevised form. Reference to that Jewish "theology," which developed in connection with the Old Testament, would undoubtedly be more valid to illustrate the background of the New Testament than references to apocryphal writings (such as Jubilees or the Testaments of the XII Patriarchs), precious though they are.

*The New Testament is not directly linked to the Old Testament. Christians inherited not only a translated Bible (LXX), but an interpreted Bible.* (The same applies to the Qumran sectaries as well. See Vermes 1969, 93). In order to evaluate the originality of the Christian message on an ethical and theological (even liturgical) level, we must ascertain what was received and assimilated. The evaluation should also include the occasions when Christianity defined its positions and expressed itself in reaction against Jewish tradition. The monumental *Setting of the Sermon on the Mount,* by W. D. Davies (1964), illustrates this situation admirably. Christians were impregnated with the traditional interpretation which they heard repeated during synagogue worship. Quotations from the Targum would come to their mind all the more easily because, according to popular custom, it was the Aramaic Targum they heard, not the Hebrew nor the Greek.

It is erroneous to imagine the New Testament authors, and Jesus himself, confronted only with the nude text of the original Bible, as we ourselves are; they received it from a living milieu, as it was understood there and then, with a whole context to orient and influence the interpretation. Even if the New Testament uses a mistaken exegesis, unconsciously or consciously (cf. Gal. 3 : 16), it is this wrong interpretation which must be taken into consideration in order to understand the New Testament. How can Hebrews 10 : 37 be explained ("He who is to come will come") if, with the author, we do not start from the misinterpretation of Habakkuk 2 : 3 in the LXX? Instead of making it apply to the coming vision, the Greek participle *erchomenos* has imported the idea of a coming one and given a messianic tone to the whole passage. Nothing would be understood of Galileo Galilei's misadventures, nor his *Eppur si muove,* without interpreting the miracle in Joshua 10 in the same way that the inquisitors did in 1633.

Let us remember that the titles of the Psalms, whatever their origin and value, are attempts at interpretation and have influenced New Testament exegesis. In *Acts* 2 : 25, Peter attributes Psalm 16 to David, and that he took this seriously is obvious from the conclusions he draws.

One can easily imagine Paul pondering on the mysterious title of Psalm 9 (LXX), "Concerning hidden things of the son," and finding there "the promise of mysterious truths about the Son" (Hanson 1974, 24; cf. Childs 1971).

This new vision of the Old Testament, seen through the prism of Tradition, includes the whole of Scripture. It is with this fresh outlook, embracing a whole body of exegetical traditions, that we too must consider such great figures as Adam, Abel, Abraham, Melchizedek, Moses, and others in order to see the relevance of their use in New Testament writings. How are we to imagine Thamar or Rahab in Matthew 1, according to the Bible or according to Tradition which canonized them? This applies also to biblical episodes that are alluded to in the New Testament. For example, the ratification of the covenant in Exodus 24 (sealed by an expiatory sacrifice, according to targumic tradition), the circumcision of the son of Moses in Exodus 4 (which had also received an expiatory significance), the brazen serpent, and so on.

New Testament typology must definitely be studied in the light of haggadic elaboration, including the Flood (1 Pet. 3:20−21), the Exodus (in 1 Cor. 10), the paschal lamb. When James 5:11 says, "You have heard of the steadfastness of Job," does that simply refer us to Job 42:10−17 or to the touched-up figure of the LXX or even to the sectarian portrait of the Qumran Job Targum or that of the Testament of Job? Anyway, the very fact that the author does not refer to Jesus himself as a model of long-suffering shows how readily one could pick up a good example in traditional folklore.

Special account must be taken of the themes connected with great Jewish feasts such as the Passover (with its connections with the Creation, the sacrifice of Isaac, and messianic eschatology [cf. Targum Exod. 12:42]), Pentecost (festival of the giving of the Law and covenantal festival), Tabernacles, Kippur, and so on. A knowledge of the themes already linked together in the Haggada would help to account for their appearance in the New Testament, thus the water and the Spirit in *J. Sukkah* V, 1 would illustrate in John 7 whose method, as pointed out by C. K. Barrett in the *Cambridge History of the Bible* (vol. 1, 406), is "to deal not so much with Old Testament texts as with Old Testament themes."

Christian authors show a certain familiarity with midrashic themes

(Gal. 4:21–31; 1 Cor. 10; 2 Cor. 3; Rom. 10:5–10), and it is easy to understand how they were able to create the Christian Midrash about Jesus as the ultimate reference in a milieu which tended to apply Scripture constantly to new situations. Modifications like "I send my messenger before *thy* face" (Luke 7:27), instead of "*My* face" in the quotation of Malachi 3:1 (probably influenced by Exodus 23:20), or the use of the expression *Christos Kyrios* ("the Messiah and Lord") in Luke 2:11 instead of "the anointed of the Lord" (*Christos Kyriou*) of the Old Testament are examples showing how, from now on, the whole of Scripture speaks of Christ.

Some New Testament statements presuppose a reading of Scripture far removed from the letter of the text, which accounts for what is said about the necessity for the sufferings of the Messiah (Matt. 16:21: "He must go to Jerusalem and suffer"), and his Resurrection on the third day "in accordance with the Scriptures" (1 Cor. 15:4; cf. Luke 24:25–27; Acts 17:3 and 26:22). The theme of the sufferings of the Messiah is strangely absent from early Jewish writings. But, if we still possessed the Targum of Isaiah 53 in its first-century recension, it might be possible to relate the Christian interpretation to an earlier Jewish tradition. In any case, the image of the suffering Moses in Acts 7 is truly that of the Haggada and could well be one of the landmarks that have survived from a former conception of the suffering Messiah. On the other hand, we should like to know which texts had been interpreted in relation to one another—for example, the connections made between Genesis 22 and Isaiah 53 (cf. Vermes 1973, 222).

On the ethical level, let us remember that in Acts 9:2 and 18:25–26 Christianity calls itself a *Way* (*hodos*). It had to establish its own *Halakah* (literally, that by which one walks, that is, rule of conduct), but not an entirely new one; and it is surprising that it was based mainly on the Old Testament and not directly on words of Jesus. It is sad to realize that it was what remained common to Jews and Christian converts from Judaism (circumcision, dietary laws, calendar) which was to be at the origin of the greatest conflicts within the Church, and created an ever wider gap between the "Church from circumcision" and the "Church from the nations," to quote the inscription on the famous fifth-century mosaic at Santa Sabina in Rome. Here again, it would be important to know more about premishnaic Jewish Halakah, an immense field, of which the biblical versions and the Midrashim do at least reveal the complexity. Too many Christian authors, with the praiseworthy intention of situating Christianity in its Jewish *Sitz im Leben*, often do not play fair when they retain only certain expressions of a ridiculous legalism by which the superiority of the New Testament is too easily proved. It is in the whole of Judaism and its Tradition (Haggada and Halakah) with its many streams, its obscurities and riches, that the Christian movement must be studied.

If one wants to understand the use of the Old Testament in the New Testament, early exegesis should be taken seriously, not because it would yield the original meaning, or would be authentic, but simply to understand its applications. It would serve no useful purpose to treat the legend of the rock which followed Israel in the desert (1 Cor. 10:4) as fanciful or puerile. On the contrary, to interpret Paul correctly, we should recall to mind many variations on this theme from Ezekiel the Tragedian (vv. 243–253), who identifies the water from the rock with the water of Elim (Exod. 15), right up to Pseudo-Philo (Biblical Ant. X, 7; XI, 15), who assimilates the water of Marah and the water of the rock; not to mention targumic and midrashic traditions. Popular identifications of biblical characters compel us to rewrite biblical history. This may have some relevance in the case of Miryam, the sister of Moses, who became the ancestor of King David, and, therefore, of the Messiah; or in the case of the two Zechariah (the priest and the prophet, 2 Chron. 24:20) identified in Targum Lamentations 2:20, a text that helps to solve the enigma of Matthew 23:35 ("Zechariah, the son of Barachiah, whom you murdered between the sanctuary and the altar"). The quoting of Psalm 69:23 in Romans 11:9 ("Let their table become a snare and a trap") takes on a completely different meaning if one presupposes that Paul had in mind the Targum rendering of the Psalm where *table* refers to the sacrifices offered to God: it is their very cult which prevents the Jews from recognizing Christ!

In short, a good New Testament exegete should react to an Old Testament text in the same way that the first Christian author did, when using it to express his faith. His first question should be: What did this text mean *for him*? The New Testament writer could rightly expect us to be familiar with "all the various Jewish customs and disputes—*zētē-*

*mata"* which Paul gave King Agrippa the credit of knowing, in order to make himself understood (Acts 26:3).

*The Gospels are largely an attempt to interpret and to apply the Scriptures to the Revelation of Christ.* It is in this application of the Scriptures that the necessity to understand them as they were then understood appears most clearly. The *demonstratio ex Scripturis* was of primary importance, at least in Palestinian Jewish milieu. As a matter of fact, we find in the New Testament 287 quotations from the Jewish Bible. In the beginning, the most conspicuous difference between Jews and Christians existed in deviating interpretations of the Old Testament.

Jesus himself adhered to an interpretative tradition, even if at times it was in order to oppose it: "You have heard . . . but I say" (Matt. 5). He taught as a *didaskalos* (teacher), and even "with authority" (Matt. 7:29), often in connection with the synagogue liturgy (Luke 4:14−28; John 6:59 and 18:20). He had to take a stand before interpretations other than his own, and occasionally suggest a new Halakah (as in Luke 14:1−6 with regard to the sabbath observance); but his language is that of the masters of that time. "He appears not to have created a single one of his basic religious terms himself" (Gerhardsson 1964, 22).

Jesus speaks and acts in relation to the hopes and conceptions of a people steeped in a religious tradition; therefore, he had of necessity to take them in the accepted meaning of the time. His way of arguing is that of the contemporary rabbis and his refutation of the Sadducees on the subject of Resurrection (Matt 22:32) is genuinely rabbinical in character, similar to that of R. Gamaliel (Sanh. 90 b) founded on Deuteronomy 4:4: "You are *all* alive this day" and "Just as you are all alive today, so shall you all live again in the world to come." I do not think J. Bonsirven (1939, 63) is fair in quoting this as an example of fanciful exegesis. Every movement in early Judaism had its own applied exegesis, and the Christian use of Scripture would be better understood if it were not isolated from contemporary systems of interpretation (for instance the Samaritan or Essene traditions). The results differ; the procedure is the same. Paul, arguing from the singular ("to your offspring—*zerâ"*) in Genesis 12:7 that Scripture means one descendant, namely Christ (Gal. 3:16), reasons in the same way as Targum and Midrash which prove, from the plural form of "blood" in Genesis 4 : 10 ("The voice of your brother's bloods cries out to me"), that Cain was the murderer also of all the righteous who should have been born to his brother (cf. Sanh. IV, 5; Koran V, 32). The famous text of Habakkuk 2 : 4, "The just man shall live by his faith," can be applied to faith in Christ in Romans 1 : 17 or to "faith in the Teacher of righteousness" in the Qumran commentary (VIII, 2−3).

Christian apologetics, in particular, had of necessity to meet the Jews on the terrain of their own interpretation; their unbelief had to be met on their own ground. How are we to understand the Christian anti-theses without first of all discovering the theses they are opposing, and finding the minimum of common ground which is essential for any discussion? Moreover, an idea as central as the fulfillment of Scripture, a typical concept in Matthew (ten examples), would be of no value if the words and life of Jesus did not fulfill all that was expected to be accomplished in the messianic and eschatological age, even in the exact details furnished by the oral Tradition. Thus it is that John 6 presents Jesus as a new Moses bringing the true bread from heaven because a repetition of the prodigies of the first Exodus was expected, that of the manna among others. If Matthew 27 : 52 speaks of a resurrection from the dead when Jesus had given up his spirit, it is probably because resurrection was connected to the messianic event. K. Stendahl (1954, 200) also remarks that the presence of the two mounts when Jesus entered Jerusalem (Matt. 21 : 5) is due to the fact that "Matthew knew a tradition which spoke about two asses" in the common messianic interpretation of Zechariah 9 : 9. Various traditions on the kind of drink offered to Jesus on the cross (wine, vinegar, wine and gall) are all to be explained by the influence of the messianic interpretation of Psalm 69. For this reason, it would be interesting to know all the passages which, in Jesus's time, were understood messianically, many having been corrected later on ac-count of anti-Christian reactions (cf. Ps. 110; Isa. 53). However the an-cient versions have preserved either simple traces (like Targum Isaiah 63 : 2, compared with Targum Genesis 49) or quite explicit passages, as in Targum Psalm 118 (the Davidic interpretation helps to understand Mark 11, 10a), Targum Genesis 49 or Targum Numbers 24 : 17.

The New Testament is largely an exegesis of the Old Testament. It chronicles the activities of Christ, who after his Resurrection appears as an interpreter of the Scriptures (Luke 24). But the thesis of the fulfillment in Jesus of the whole plan of salvation had to be integrated into contemporary conceptions of sacred history. One is aware of this through the considerable influence of apocalyptic ideas on the New Testament texts. Jesus himself had to take a stand with regard to certain conceptions of messianic eschatology: "And you, who do you say that I am?" (Matt. 16:15). The same applies to Qumran: the *pesharim* show how the sect understood the development of sacred history (cf. commentary on Ps. 37) and how they saw their situation and role in it. For a proper understanding of these biblical commentaries, it is as important to take into account these presupposed ideas as to find out the historical situation which the interpreter claims to explain.

In this context, let us remember the question of the so-called Testimonies (collections of messianic proof texts). It is obvious that the choice of these Testimonies, intended for controversy or for teaching, presupposes an exegesis which reflects Christian tenets as much as conceptions of the Jews for whom they were intended. This grouping of texts (a practice now confirmed by Qumran texts) results from motivations which can be discerned only in the broader context of their traditional interpretation. It presupposes Midrash or previous exegesis, and it is no surprise to see this word introduce the pesher of Psalm 1:1 in 4 Q 174 (Florilegium).

Every passage of Scripture was subjected to thorough investigation. Acts 17 describes a confrontation with the Jews of Beroea who "had welcomed the [Christian] message with great enthusiasm [and] each day examined the Scriptures to see whether these things were so." This is an allusion to midrashic activity, as no doubt is the use of the verb *ereunān* (to search the Scriptures) in John 5:39 and 7:52.

Where can we expect to find the principles and thought patterns which guided the elaboration of specifically Christian conceptions on the Old Testament basis except by going as deeply as possible into Jewish Tradition, in so far as it is possible to recapture it from this early period?

*The history of the development of the New Testament, right up to its final redaction, could be illuminated in all its stages by phenomena well known in Jewish Tradition.* Together with the problem of transmission studied by Birger Gerhardsson (1961), the transmission of haggadic tradition reveals a uniformity of content side by side with a constant variety of formulations as L. Zunz pointed out so long ago (1832) in reference to Haggadah in general. It would be rewarding to compare the question of longer and shorter redactions of the Beatitudes and the Our Father in Matthew and Luke with certain targumic paraphrases of which several recensions are still extant (as Exod. 12:42 or Gen. 2 and 22). M. McNamara (1966, 142−45) has, unfortunately, devoted only a few pages of his book to this interesting question which merits deeper study. It is true that study of the literary forms, genres, and structures in midrashic literature is only beginning, but significant steps have already been made (cf. the work of J. Heinemann). The facts that McNamara points out are indeed relevant for the synoptic problem: same paraphrase in lesser or greater details; fixed paraphrase, different order; same concept expressed in different terms.

For the form of the Old Testament quotations in the New Testament, it should be remembered that, in oral controversy, the texts came to mind under a "targumized" form. Moreover, it was not the letter but the meaning of the passage that had to be given. But at the time of redaction there was a tendency to return to the letter of Scripture, keeping the "targumisms" only when the point of the discussion demanded it. It is some time since A. Baumstark (1956) showed that some phenomena of transformation and adaptation of Old Testament texts in the New Testament had their parallels in the Targum (cf. Gundry 1967, 173).

We know today that first-century Judaism was much more variegated than imagined by former historians, who projected backward the monolithic image of Rabbinic Judaism. It must also be admitted that in the Haggadah, for instance, there must have been a much freer interchange of ideas among the different parties. A certain analogy in exegetical methods must certainly have existed, and Qumran has already taught us much about early Jewish hermeneutics. In any case, if recourse to the Old Testament to explain the New Testament has characterized an important turning point in modern scholarship, it is still true that to concentrate only on the literal meaning of the biblical text is myopia. New Testament exegetes know that they have to reckon with a complex background; and particularly in the use of the Old Testament in the New

Testament, they must have recourse to a variety of hypotheses to give an explanation of the facts.

The Bible being the chart of Jewish life, it is in its interpretation that the historian will also find the information he needs to penetrate into the soul of early Judaism. G. Vermes (in *Cambridge History of the Bible*, vol. 1, p. 229) offers one of the best statements on the importance of Judaism to the study of Christianity. I conclude with his statement. "Since the Christian *kerygma* was first formulated by Jews for Jews, using Jewish arguments and methods of exposition, it goes without saying that a thorough knowledge of contemporary Jewish exegesis is essential to the understanding (and not just a better understanding) of the message of the New Testament and, even more, of Jesus."

## Literature Cited

Baumstark, A. "Die zitate des Mt.-Evanseliums aus dem zwölfprophetenbuch." *Biblica* 37 (1956): 296–313.

Bonsirven, J. *Exegese rabbinique et exegese paulinienne*. Paris, 1939.

Brownlee, W. H. "Biblical Interpretation among the Sectaries of the Dead Sea Scrolls." *Biblical Archaeologist* 14 (1951): 54–76.

Charles, R. H. *The Apocrypha and Pseudepigrapha of the O. T.* Vol. 2.

Childs, B. S. "Psalm Titles and Midrashic Exegesis." *Journal of Semitic Studies* 16 (1971): 137–50.

Cross, Frank Moore. "History of the Biblical Text in the Light of Discoveries in the Judaean Desert." *Harvard Theological Review* 57 (1964): 281–299.

Daube, D. *The H. T. and Rabbinic Judaism*. London, 1956.

Dentan, R. *The Apocrypha, Bridge of the Testaments*. New York, 1964.

Geiger, A. *Urschrift und Uebersetzungen der Bibel*. Frankfort am Main, 1928.

Gerhardsson, B. *Memory and Manuscript*. Uppsala, 1961.

———. *Tradition and Transmission in Early Christianity*. Lund, 1964.

Gertner, Meir. "Midrashim in the New Testament." *Journal of Semitic Studies* 7 (1962): 292.

Gundry, R. H. *The Use of the O. T. in St. Matthew's Gospel*. Leiden, 1967.

Hanson, Anthony T. *Studies in Paul's Technique and Theology*. London, 1974.

Harris, Rendel. *Expos. Times* 32 (1920–21): 374.

Lieberman, S. *Hellenism in Jewish Palestine*. New York, 1962.

McNamara, M. *The N. T. and the Palestinian Targum to the Pentateuch*. Rome, 1966.

Manson, T. W. *Journal of Theological Studies* 46 (1945): 135.

Pfeiffer, Robert H. *Introduction to the O. T.* New York, 1948.

Prijs, L. *Judische Tradition in der Septuaginta.* Leiden, 1948.

Purvis, James D. *The Samaritan Pentateuch and the Origin of the Samaritan Sect.* Cambridge, Mass., 1968.

Slomovic, E. *Revue de Qumran* 7 (1969): 3–15.

Stendahl, K. *The School of St. Matthew.* Lund, 1954.

Vermes, G. *Annual of Leeds University Oriental Society.* Vol. 6. Leiden, 1969.

———. *Scripture and Tradition in Judaism.* Leiden, 1973.

# Sons of God and Ecclesia: An Intertestamental Analysis

HARALD RIESENFELD

IN THE KING JAMES' BIBLE of 1611, which is the well-known Authorized Version, the seventh beatitude has been rendered in the following way: "Blessed are the peacemakers: for they shall be called the children of God" (Matt. 5:9). We shall not discuss at great length the point that the translation *peacemakers* does not do justice to the underlying Greek. The Greek word *eirēnopoioi*, if translated literally, does mean "makers of peace." But the element *makers* had by the time of the New Testament lost its active sense, and therefore the adequate translation is rather "keepers of peace," or "those who keep peace." Other sayings in the Sermon on the Mount illustrate what is meant by "keepers of peace." One is, "You have heard the commandment, An eye for an eye, a tooth for a tooth. But what I say to you is: offer no resistance to injury. When a person strikes you on the right cheek, turn and offer him the other. If anyone wants to go to law over your shirt, hand him your coat as well. . . . Love your enemies, pray for your persecutors" (Matt. 5:38–40, 44). Another is St. Paul's transformation of the seventh beatitude, perhaps the earliest commentary on that saying of Jesus. "Never repay injury with injury. . . . If possible, live peaceably with everyone. . . . Do not be conquered by evil but conquer evil with good" (Rom. 12:17–21). Jesus does not think of peacemakers as officers of the

United Nations traveling to other countries in order to reconcile nations or their leaders. Far from that, he thinks of his disciples as living peacefully and patiently in a world where the right of might seems to prevail.

Of greater interest in our present context is the fact that the Revised Standard Version and all other more recent translations do not read "children of God" but "sons of God." When the wording *sons of God* was introduced into the new Swedish translation of the New Testament, many readers reacted negatively and accused the translators of overzealous literalism and sex discrimination. As a matter of fact, the Greek text reads "sons of God" in the seventh beatitude as well as in other sayings of Jesus. Only outside the synoptic Gospels, in the Pauline and Johannine letters and twice in the Fourth Gospel, the Greek text has the equivalent of "children of God," for example, "See what love the Father has bestowed on us, in letting us be called children of God! Yet that is what we are" (1 John 3 : 1). The translation "children of God" instead of "sons of God" in the sayings of Jesus seems to go back to Luther and has been preserved in Lutheran translations of the New Testament until this time. Probably Luther felt that "children of God" sounded more intimate than "sons of God"—he was often sentimental.

The reason *sons of God* is the appropriate rendering and is rightly chosen by all ambitious modern translations of the sayings of Jesus is by no means an inclination to mere literalism. There are more substantial arguments, and that is what we shall now look into.

There are other instances in the synoptic Gospels in which Jesus speaks of the sons of God. The Sadducees were questioning Jesus about the resurrection of the dead—this party within the Jewish people in New Testament times did not believe in a resurrection—and asked him what would happen on the last day to seven brothers who had successively married the same woman without leaving her any children. In the Lucan version of this narrative Jesus replied: "The children of this age marry and are given in marriage but those judged worthy of a place in the age to come and of resurrection from the dead do not. They become like angels and are no longer liable to death. Sons of the resurrection, they are sons of God" (Luke 20:34–36). In other words, when they rise from the dead and death is no longer threatening them, they will become like angels and will be sons of God. Here it is clearly stated that sons of God are something that human beings are not in their present life on earth but will become in the age to come. It is an eschatological concept, a statement which envisages a final destiny after the end events of history.

The same aspect can be found in a saying of Jesus in the Lucan counterpart to the Sermon on the Mount in Matthew. "Love your enemy and do good; lend without expecting repayment. Then will your recompense be great. You will rightly be called sons of the Most High" (Luke 6:35). Those who love their enemy and do good are, as we have seen, the ones who in the Matthean beatitudes are called those who keep peace. But here in Luke we realize that being called sons of God is a great recompense, something which is not yet present but belongs to the age to come. Also in this context, *sons of God* is an eschatological concept.

Now, what does the term *sons of God* mean, where does it come from, and why has it been used by Jesus? The answer is not given by the Gospels but can be found in the Old Testament. The writings of the Old Testament, in their different stages, provide means to follow a fascinating line of development in the use of the term *sons of God,* prior to its occurrence in the Gospels.

The most illustrative text, with regard to our problem, is Psalm 89. In its introductory part the greatness of God is emphasized. No one in his heavenly court can equal him. "The heavens proclaim your wonders, O Lord, and your faithfulness in the assembly of the holy ones. For who in the skies can rank with the Lord? Who is like the Lord among the sons of God? God is terrible in the council of the holy ones; he is great and awesome beyond all around him" (Ps. 89:6–8). The traditional translation *sons of God* obscures the fact that the Hebrew text reads "the sons of the gods." Here we have a reminiscence of a primeval polytheistic conception of the heavenly world: Yahweh, the God of Israel, was surrounded by other gods, the gods of the nations, but they were inferior to him. In the course of time, with the rise of an exclusive monotheistic concept of God, the passage has come to be interpreted in such a way that the subordinate gods are depreciated and considered angels surrounding and serving the only true God.

There are, however, other passages in the Old Testament in which the original implication of the sons of the gods can still be found. In Genesis 6:1–2 we read that the sons of the gods saw how beautiful the daughters of men were, and they got children with them, the heroes of old. (Here the RSV translates *sons of God,* the NAB *sons of heaven.*) This narrative is obviously a remnant of a more elaborate myth about a celestial pantheon, and the same can be said of a passage in the Psalms. "God arises in the divine assembly, he judges in the midst of the gods . . . I [God] said: You are gods, and all of you sons of the Most High" (Ps. 82:1, 6; cf. John 10:34). The pantheon has in the last-mentioned text been transformed into a heavenly scene of judgment in which Yahweh judges other gods because they have performed their assignments of divine rulership in an unsatisfactory way. But to the degree that the power of Yahweh is heightened, the role of the heavenly beings around him is degraded. Behind the wording of Deuteronomy 32:8, "He set up boundaries of the peoples after the number of the sons of God," lies the idea—made clear by a fragment of the Dead Sea Scrolls found at Qumran—that the sons of God are leaders or angels in command of their peoples. In the book of Job (1:6; 2:1; 38:7) and Daniel (3:25 [92]), which are from Hellenistic times, the sons of God have been definitely domesticated into angels. What has to be retained from these texts in the Old Testament in which the sons of God appear is the idea that sons of God are beings who live in the immediate presence of God and are members of the heavenly assembly that surrounds the throne of God.

In the period following the return from exile in Babylon, the fifth to third centuries B.C., a development took place within Jewish religion that was to change, in a radical way, the concept of man and the ideas about man's destiny. According to Israelite thought in earlier, classic times, death was considered the separation of man from God; it was not the annihilation of the individual. The souls of the dead went down to Sheol, the netherworld, where they maintained a dim, shadowy existence, far away from God and the heavenly world. As a psalm of lament and affliction puts it: "My life draws near to the nether world. I am numbered with those who go down into the pit; I am a man without strength. My couch is among the dead, like the slain who lie in the grave, whom you remember no longer and who are cut off from your care" (Ps. 88:3–6).

A totally different perspective opens in those writings in the Old Testament that are called Wisdom Literature. These books reflect characteristic changes that Jewish thought underwent in Hellenistic times, not without influences from Greek civilization in the dynamic centuries before and after Alexander the Great.

In the book of Wisdom, written in Greek, probably at Egyptian Alexandria some hundred years before the coming of Christ, we find a description of the final judgment. When it arrives, the wicked will witness what happens to the just man, whose death had been to them a matter of contempt. "They see the death of the wise man and do not understand what the Lord intended for him" (Wisd. 4:17). But at the judgment the wicked will change their opinion about the just man and say, rueful and groaning through anguish of spirit: "This is he whom once we held as a laughingstock and as a type for mockery. His life we accounted madness, and his death dishonoured. See how he is accounted among the sons of God, how his lot is with the holy ones!" (Wisd. 5:3–5). The wicked finally have to realize that those on earth who lived insignificant or despised lives gain an entrance into the heavenly world.

As we can see from this text, the idea has been accepted in Jewish thought that the righteous, at the end of their life on earth, are not doomed to descend into the shadow of death, into an existence withdrawn from God. Rather, they are taken up to stand before the face of God, in his immediate presence. For the righteous, death is not a separation from God and from a life worth living, but rather a way to the nearness of God and to the fullness of life. The image of the heavenly assembly to which the righteous man now has access has beyond doubt been taken from texts such as Psalms 89:6ff. Both there and in Wisdom 5:5 we meet the sons of God and the holy ones (or saints). The departed righteous receives his place in a life-to-come among the sons of God and the holy ones.

More than likely, one of the impulses to change Jewish ideas about the final destiny of man came from the story of Elijah being taken up to heaven by a whirlwind (2 Kings 2:9–14). In this text from a time long before the Babylonian exile, the basic idea is inherent that God does not abandon a pious and faithful servant when he reaches the end of his life on earth. Human life in accordance with the will of God has its goal not in a separation from God but in the presence of God. The narrative of the ascension of Elijah forms a model of thought that cannot have remained without effect.

The passage quoted from Wisdom 5 is only one sample of a broader pattern. The deceased wise and just man is not only counted among the sons of God, but he has also found his lot with the holy ones, both of these categories originally belonging to the heavenly court of Yahweh. The holy ones or saints in older layers of the Old Testament writings are similar to the sons of God, divine beings who were gradually transformed into angels. "Call now! Will anyone respond to you? To which of the holy ones will you appeal?" (Job 5:1) The holy ones had evidently been invoked in the past, when they still were gods. "In his holy ones God places no confidence" (Job 15:15), now that they have been degraded (cf. Dan. 4:10, 14, 20). Finally in Daniel 7, the holy ones or saints of the Most High have become the chosen people of God who have to endure on earth tests and sufferings on their way to the heavenly kingdom, where they will find their proper place in the presence of God (Dan. 7:23–27). The title "holy ones of the Most High" also appears in the Damascus Document, a text closely related to the writings of the Qumran sectarians (CD 20:8).

Another passage in the book of Wisdom is relevant to the present discussion. There it is said, "If the just one be the son of God, he [God] will defend him" (2:18). And the argument of the wicked, who reject immortality, goes on. "With revilement and torture let us put him to the test that we may see proof of his gentleness and try his patience. Let us condemn him to a shameful death; for according to his own words, God will take care of him" (2:19, 20). In these verses the pattern of the holy ones in Daniel 7 reappears. The wicked claim that God shall vindicate the righteous man during his life on earth, whereas the teachers of wisdom knew that "son of God" is a quality of life to be gained only by a vindication posterior to death. Only in a world to come will it become apparent who the sons of God are. In 2 Maccabees 7:34 the righteous martyrs who are facing their execution are called "children of heaven," a wording which seems to anticipate, for those who deliberately endure suffering and death, the final dignity or status of the sons of God (cf. 1 Enoch 101:1).

Several passages in the Wisdom Literature and in the Greek translation of the writings of the Old Testament, usually called the Septuagint, show that pious circles in the Jewish people during the centuries preceding the time of Christ tried to find support in the original Hebrew writings of the Old Testament for the idea of a final destination in heaven for those who had led a righteous and wise life on earth and who had been willing to take upon them the sufferings and privations of such a life. Hence, while the Masoretic (i.e., Hebrew) text of Proverbs 9 : 10 reads, "The beginning of wisdom is the fear of the Lord, and knowledge of the Holy One is understanding," the Septuagint gives, "The council of the holy ones has understanding." The translators—or rather the teachers of Jewish wisdom in their environment—were anxious to prove, by means of slight alterations of the sense of the underlying Hebrew text, that there is a council, a congregation of holy ones in heaven, something to look forward to for pious Jews. This was evidently more interesting than the thought expressed in the original text, namely that true knowledge is a result of the study of Scripture. This emancipated method of interpreting a scriptural passage was in no way unusual and can be found here and there in the Pauline epistles. Likewise, the statement in the book of Sirach that Zerubbabel and Jeshua, Jozadah's son, erected the holy temple destined for everlasting glory has been changed in one of the manuscripts to mean that they raised for the Lord a people (*laos* instead of *naos*) destined for everlasting glory (49 : 12). The Greek verb *to raise* indicates in this context that "everlasting glory" is to be interpreted in a clearly eschatological sense.

When viewed against this background the meaning of the term *sons of God* in the sayings of Jesus becomes clear. What has not yet been observed is the fact that *sons of God* is a traditional image which has been loaded, in the centuries preceding the time of Christ, with an eschatological content, as exemplified in Jesus's reply to the question of the Sadducees. "Those worthy of a place in the age to come and of resurrection do not marry. They become like angels and are no longer liable to death. Sons of the resurrection, they are sons of God" (Luke 20 : 35 f.). All elements of this saying fit into the same pattern: no longer liable to death, a place in the age to come, like angels, sons of God. The only aspect which in some way is new in this context is that of resurrection. In Jewish thought in New Testament times there was no consistent idea of how the translation from this life to the life of a new age would occur. Different images or perspectives were used side by side: imminent judgment, coming of a Messiah and of a new age, immortality of the soul, and resurrection of the dead who sleep in the dust of the earth.

With the help of the religious language of his time and of originally mythological images, Jesus is able to make clear that life after death will be characterized by totally new qualities: it will be a transformed life in the presence of God. Therefore the problem of the procreation of off-spring, made necessary by death and thus confined to a world where death reigns, will no more exist. The term *sons of God* is apparently the signal that announces and opens the perspective in which a phrase like Jesus's reply to the Sadducees has to be considered. Whenever the sons of God appear, it is a question of a new life beyond death, a transformed life in the nearness of God. At the same time we can be sure that the term *sons of God* has formed part of the original teaching of Jesus. It fits in a perfect way the pictorial language, rooted in Old Testament tradition, which Jesus preferably used when formulating central parts of his eschatological message. No transmitter of the gospel tradition, in the time of the early Church, would have been interested in putting an enigmatic metaphor like *sons of God* into the sayings of Jesus.

The use of pictorial, originally mythological, language in the proclamation of Jesus can suitably be illustrated by a reference to the well-known phrase "the kingdom of heaven." The occurrence of this expression is restricted to the sayings of Jesus in the Gospel of Matthew. It corresponds to "kingdom of God" which is used in the other Gospels. The fact that Matthew in thirty-four cases out of thirty-eight has "kingdom of heaven" instead of "kingdom of God" is generally explained by a reference to the fact that Matthew is addressing his gospel to Jews or Jewish Christians who would avoid uttering the name of God and were accustomed to replace it by a periphrasis such as *heaven*. This explanation, though, cannot be correct. For in this case Matthew would have refrained from using it also in the four instances where it occurs in the First Gospel. Moreover he would have avoided the name of God in other combinations where he writes it out without restriction. The true explanation seems to be that Matthew has preserved the original mythological and pictorial expression that Jesus had used himself. According to Daniel 7, a text which was of first-rate importance to Jesus, a kingdom was ready in heaven, prepared by God and awaiting the Son of Man (Dan. 7:13 f.) as well as the holy ones of the Most High (Dan. 7:27). Jesus might well have spoken of the kingdom of God also, and when the proclamation of the Christian message was addressed to the Greco-

Roman world, the time had come to substitute definitely the term *kingdom of God* for *kingdom of heaven*. The allusions to Daniel 7 inherent in the latter term would not have been comprehensible to those living in a non-Jewish environment.

Finally, we have reached the passage in the gospels where the expression *sons of God* is most conspicuous and has proved to be most enigmatic, the passage from which we started the present investigation. We are now returning to the seventh beatitude: "Blessed are those who keep peace: they shall be called the sons of God" (Matt. 5:9). The obstacle with which commentators have usually been struggling is the fact that this saying as well as all other beatitudes have been interpreted in an inner-worldly perspective. Those who live a peaceful life—or even make peace in the sense that they reconcile men to men and man to God—will please God and be acceptable to him. This sense of the term *sons of God* has been derived from the use of the term *children of God* in some of the epistles. So Dummelow writes in his well-known commentary: "Children [(RV "sons") of God] Because in this aspect they are especially like their heavenly Father, who has sent peace and goodwill down to earth in the person of His dear Son." Having dealt, however, with the term *sons of God* in Old Testament texts, especially in the Wisdom Literature, we know that it is part of a definitely eschatological concept. "They shall be called the sons of God." The logical subject which underlies the passive form of the verb *to call* is God. Moreover the verb stands in the future form. When will God call the peaceful sons of God? He will call them at the moment when hope is being fulfilled on the threshold of the age to come, in a transcendent world where the presence of God is conspicuous. Calling the peaceful the sons of God means admitting them to a place near his heavenly throne, a picture which necessarily has to be demythologized in a legitimate way. What comes out is a life set free from sufferings and restrictive boundaries, not least those that men impose upon their fellowmen, a life in its fullness, free from death, in unbroken interrelations with other human beings and in the nearness of God.

It has often been forgotten that all beatitudes have in fact the same eschatological structure. What Jesus promises to his listeners will not be realized in this world. This is obvious from the sixth beatitude: "Blessed are the single-hearted: for they shall see God" (Matt. 5:8). This will never be possible in the present world; no cultic purity can grant access to a place where God can be seen. And when in the third beatitude the land is promised to the lowly (Matt. 5 : 5), it is in no way a question of the earth in the ordinary sense of the word, but rather of a new earth, succeeding together with new heavens when the former earth passes away (Rev. 21 : 1). Saying that the lowly shall inherit the land, Jesus must have thought of the promises of past times granting the land to the people of Israel, promises which already the Prophets had interpreted in an eschatological sense, for example, in Isaiah 61 : 7: "Since their shame was double and disgrace and spittle were their portion, they shall love a double inheritance in their land, everlasting joy shall be theirs" (cf. Ps. 37 : 11).

The seventh beatitude, promising those who keep peace to be called the sons of God, is like all other beatitudes—paradoxical. Their original setting can be indicated in the following way. When preaching the gospel of the kingdom, Jesus turned his attention to those who had followed him and listened to his words. They did not belong to the establishment of the Jewish people but had their place among those who called themselves the poor or the humble and were looked down upon as the lot that knows nothing about the law and therefore were considered lost and cursed (John 7 : 49). To them, against all expectation, was addressed the promise that the kingdom belonged to them and would be inherited by them. Their present life was filled with suffering and humiliation; hunger and thirst and tears were their lot. But one day they would reach the goal of their longing. All things would be radically changed; kingship and dominion and majesty would be given to them; for they were no less than the holy ones of the Most High, the holy, God-chosen people described in the prophecy of Daniel (Dan. 7 : 25, 27). But there was only one way to this final consummation: the way in the footsteps of the Son of Man. "If a man wishes to come after me, he must deny his very self, take up his cross and begin to follow in my steps. Whoever would save his life will lose it, but whoever loses his life for my sake will find it" (Matt. 16 : 24–25).

The eschatological perspective which is predominant in the beatitudes is applicable, in the same way, to that saying of Jesus which has been quoted earlier. "Love your enemy and do good; lend without expecting repayment. Then will your recompense be great. You will rightly be called sons of the Most High" (Luke 6:35). This saying is equally paradoxical. Self-denying is like losing one's own life. But it will result in a reward that transcends the limits of the present age. Those who sacrifice their selfish intentions will gain, in a world to come, a life characterized by the traditional metaphor *sons of God*.

In the Matthean passage parallel to the sayings from Luke 6:35 already quoted, a modification of the expression *sons of God* has been introduced. There we read: "Love your enemies, pray for your persecutors. Then you will become sons of your heavenly Father" (Matt. 5:44–45). The notion "sons of your heavenly Father," though obviously derived from "sons of God," seems to have lost its eschatological flavor and expresses most likely, as the context shows, the consciousness of being dependent upon God, who according to the teaching of Jesus accepts to be called Father. Thus "sons of your heavenly Father" does not designate what a follower of Jesus will be in the age to come but what he is already in this world. The eschatological outlook has been changed into a sentiment of security under the protection of God. The question is whether Jesus himself has made this change or whether it is a transposition of a metaphor which has been made by the evangelist or an earlier transmitter of the gospel tradition. It does not seem plausible that Jesus would have deprived a pictorial expression of its eschatological signification.

The outlook on an age to come has been abandoned and attention is being focused on the status of a Christian when the expression *children of God* is used in the letters of Paul and in the Johannine writings. Especially the Fourth Gospel and the First Epistle of John have developed the term *children of God* to designate the confident relationship with God that Christians experience during their earthly life. Curiously, the achievement reached in the present situation is viewed against the background of a final consummation: "Dearly beloved, we are God's children now, what we shall later be has not yet come to light" (John 3:2); or "Any who did accept him he empowered to become children of God" (John 1:12). As for the phrase, "See what love the Father has bestowed on us in letting us be called children of God" (John 3:1), it is remarkably similar to the seventh beatitude in its latter part, with the exception that the futurist perspective has been replaced by a presentist one.

There is no doubt that St. Paul was familiar with those sayings of Jesus that use the term *sons of God*. Otherwise he would not have been able to understand and to apply the term in exactly the same sense as Jesus did. This observation is one of the proofs we possess of the fact that Paul had received and knew the gospel tradition, obviously in its oral stage.

In a most interesting section of his letter to the Romans, Paul plays off the term *children of God* against the traditional, mythological term *sons of God*. By means of the former, more sentimental term he indicates what Christian believers already are in their relation to a heavenly Father in the present time. With the help of the latter term, *sons of God,* he makes clear what Christians will be transformed into, in the age to come, at the return of Christ in his heavenly glory. This dialectical confrontation of two different aspects of Christian life has hitherto not been adequately understood by those who have commented upon the passage in question.

Thus Paul writes in Romans 8 : 14–19, "All who are led by the Spirit of God are sons of God." That means that Christians who have received the gift of the Spirit are on their way to a final goal in heaven, as are the holy ones in Daniel 7, and that their way leads through sufferings. Paul continues, "You did not receive a spirit of slavery leading you back into fear, but a spirit of adoption through which we cry out: 'Abba!' [Father]." God has adopted those who believe to become sons of God, in the likeness of Christ, who is the Son of God, and therefore they can call God Abba, Father, just as Christ did. Paul goes on: "The Spirit himself gives witness with our spirit that we are children of God" (that is to say: already in the present time). "But if we are children [already in our present situation], we are heirs as well, heirs of God, heirs with Christ." Here we ask, what are the Christians to inherit? And the answer is, the kingdom of God, the kingdom which still is in heaven. This kingdom has been given to Christ; we shall be heirs with him, becoming sons of God as he is *the* Son of God. Yet, there is one condition, familiar to us from Daniel 7 and from the sayings of Jesus, "if only we suffer with him [Christ] so as to be glorified with him."

And Paul concludes, "I consider the sufferings of the present to be as nothing compared with the glory to be revealed and given to us" (not revealed in us). "Indeed the whole created world eagerly waits for the moment when the sons of God will be revealed" (and that means that those who are now on their way will be able to join the heavenly company of the sons of God).

There is the same outlook in the beatitudes addressed by Jesus to his followers and in that chapter of the letter to the Romans in which Paul speaks of the glory to be revealed and given to those who are in Christ Jesus. Salvation is transcendental; release from suffering and privation cannot be reached in this life and the present world. The return of Christ and the establishment of a new age, implying new conditions of life, is to be waited for with endurance and self-denial.

It is typical of Paul that not only does he take over from the sayings of Jesus an image such as "sons of God" but also reflects on it and works out new aspects when he uses the term in his exposition of Christian hope. Those who listened to Jesus, when he was sitting on the mountainside north of the Sea of Galilee, were invited to have confidence in the person of him who taught them. Paul, being the apostle of the Risen Christ, referred to the Spirit anticipating and prefiguring the transforming power of the age to come. "The Spirit himself gives witness with our spirit that we are children of God" (Rom. 8:16). This spiritual experience is the warrant of the Christian hope in the time lying between the earthly life of Jesus and the return of the heavenly Christ.

What has not been observed hitherto is the fact that the images of the sons of God—the heavenly company surrounding the throne of God—and of the holy ones—the chosen people on its way to a heavenly kingdom—are closely related to the idea of the ecclesia, the Church. In a large number of books and articles written during the last hundred years, scholars have discussed the question of where the term *ecclesia,* as it is used in the writings of the New Testament, has been derived or taken over from. This problem has remained a riddle, though, and no plausible solution has been found. Two answers have been proposed, and New Testament students have had to resort to accepting, more or less half-heartedly, one of them.

One explanation is that the idea of the Christian ecclesia has been derived from the assembly of the Israelite people in the presence of the Lord. The ideal model in the Old Testament is the proclamation of the Law at Mount Sinai. In Exodus 19:17 and following, we are told that Moses led the people out of the camp to meet God, and they stationed themselves at the foot of the mountain. When Moses, having been summoned to the top of the mountain, went down to the people again, he proclaimed to them the commands of the Lord. In later times, when the people had settled in the country given to them, it was not easy in practice to gather an assembly of all Israelites. But in theory, war as well as worship and the promulgation of laws as well as the enthronement of kings were matters to be handled by the whole of the people gathered in a solemn assembly, *qahal* (sometimes *'edah*). This idea is present in the Psalms: "Let them extol him in the assembly of the people and praise him in the council of the elders" (Ps. 107:32); and, "Sing to the Lord a new song of praise in the assembly of the faithful" (Ps. 149:1). In the Septuagint *ekklēsia* stands for the Hebrew *qahal,* the assembly of the people in its entirety. And to Philo, the Jewish writer in the first century A.D., the idea of the people of Israel being gathered in a holy assembly during the time of their march through the desert is still familiar.

Admittedly the early church, not unlike the sectarians of Qumran, considered itself the new and true people of God. However, the idea that it took over the term *ekklēsia* from the Old Testament *qahal,* is made less credible by the fact that the assembly of Israel was an abstract entity in a remote past or a stereotyped phenomenon, when it sometimes was made part of the hope facing a restoration in messianic times.

An alternative background to the concept of the ecclesia are the conventions of citizens in Greek communities, or the gatherings in Jewish synagogues, which originated in the time following the return from the Babylonian exile. To these the Greek term *ekklēsia* is equally applicable. The meetings held in the synagogues were certainly considered, in some way, solemn and exclusive. But it is hard to believe that early Christians would have considered their communion a mere analogy to civic assemblies in Greek cities or to the various synagogues that existed in Jerusalem and in other places where a Jewish population lived.

However, another solution to our problem can be found. No attention has been paid to the fact that precisely the term *ekklēsia* appears in the Septuagint translation of Psalm 89, the psalm which provides the key to the understanding of the term *sons of God.* There we read, in the passage already quoted: "The heavens proclaim your wonders, O Lord, and your faithfulness, in the assembly of the holy ones. . . . Who is like the Lord among the sons of God?" (Ps. 89:6–7). Once again we have to realize that this text describes the heavenly court of Yahweh, and in the Greek translation of the Septuagint the word for assembly is precisely *ekklēsia*. Gathered in heaven in the presence of God is the assembly of celestial beings, holy ones and sons of God, originally inferior deities who were in the course of time degraded to angels. In the book of Sirach, Wisdom sings her own praises in the assembly (*ekklēsia*) of the Most High (Sir. 24:1–2). Finally, in the development of Jewish thought righteous men were admitted to that heavenly assembly after their deaths.

Now things become clearer. The combination of assembly (*ekklēsia*) and holy ones in Psalm 89:6 decides the matter. We know that the early Christians called themselves holy ones—a better translation than "saints," which makes us think of the signification this word acquired later on in the Church. The Christians called themselves holy ones because they were convinced that they were God's chosen people on their way to the kingdom awaiting them in heaven. There they would form part of God's assembly.

It is evident why Paul uses the term *ecclesia of God*. Although considering themselves the true Israel, early Christians never speak of the new ecclesia of Israel. The ecclesia of God is the heavenly assembly gathered in the presence of God. In local Christian communities God's heavenly ecclesia is anticipated and to a certain extent made visible. Therefore the second letter to the Corinthians is addressed "to the church of God that is at Corinth, and to all the holy ones of the church who live in Achaia" (2 Cor. 1:1). There is only one church, the church of God, which is manifested in those places where a Christian community exists. The plural form, *ekklēsiai*, is a later derivative (e.g., 1 Cor. 7:17; 11:16; 14:34). Likewise the expression *church of Christ* (Rom. 16:23) is a later formation.

The Christian ecclesia consists of holy ones, as does the heavenly assembly in Psalm 89:6, thus Paul speaks of the ecclesiae of the holy ones (1 Cor. 14:34). Because the ecclesia has its real place in an otherworldliness and in the presence of God, the apostle can say: "We have our home-land in heaven" [which is a more adequate translation than "citizenship"] and from there we eagerly await the coming of our Saviour, the Lord Jesus Christ. He will give a new form to this lowly body of ours and remake it according to the pattern of his glorified body" (Phil. 3:20–21). A transformation is needed before the chosen ones will reach their final destination. But already in their present situation the members of a Christian community are apostrophized as follows: "Now you are fellow citizens of the holy ones [the celestial assembly] and fellow members of the household of God" (which has its proper place in heaven [Eph. 2:19]).

In this way "kingdom of God" and "ecclesia of God" are parallel concepts, supplementing one another. Both of them express, by means of pictorial or metaphorical language, a transcendental reality. In both cases this transcendental reality is anticipated in the present situation of the Christian community. The kingdom of God exercises its power wherever the gospel is preached. The ecclesia of God assumes shape wherever a Christian community exists and functions.

Examining the Old Testament background of the terms *sons of God* and *ecclesia* and their use in the writings of the New Testament, we have seen that they both can be properly understood only if they are viewed in an eschatological perspective. That means that an inner-worldly exposition does justice neither to the beatitudes nor to the idea of the Church in early Christianity. Both Jesus and the Christian teachers in the Apostolic age were looking forward to a radical change, the end of the present age, the final judgment and a transformation making all things new (Rev. 21:5). This has sometimes been forgotten or put aside in biblical studies in recent times. When Jesus proclaimed the gospel of the kingdom of God and when the apostles preached faith in Jesus Christ, they declared that human life will get its fulfillment and final destination only beyond the limits of space and time, in the beatific presence of God.

# The Hermeneutic Circle—
## Uses and Abuses in Translating the Bible

HARALD RIESENFELD

LORD RUSSEL (1872–1970) once maintained that the word *cheese* would not be understood by a person who had never, in a nonlinguistic way—that is, by eyesight, taste, smell or perception of touch—been in contact with the so-named dairy product. In order to have an idea of what a cheese is like, you should have tasted or at least seen or scented a real cheese.

Against this, Roman Jacobson, a well-known philologist in the field of Slavonic languages, asserted that with the help of words and objects such as *whey* and *curd* you could make clear to people in a cheeseless civilization what cheese is like. Moreover, he pointed out that we are able to grasp the meaning and have pleasant associations in our minds when we hear or read words like *nectar* and *ambrosia*. We can appreciate what they designate without ever having tasted their exquisite flavor or without having made the acquaintance of the divine consumers of these delicacies.

Anyone who translates biblical writings for his own use or for other people continually meets with conceptions, things and ideas, which he has never personally experienced. Yet he soon feels familiar with them, at least so that he can understand the words in their proper context. Nobody has ever been in heaven, not the astronauts from east or west and not even St. Paul when he refers to a man who was caught up to the third heaven (2 Cor. 12:2). Nevertheless, the biblical writers knew fairly well what they meant when they used the word *heaven,* and we, for our part, understand without difficulty what they intended to say when using this word.

In his accounts of the Ascension, Luke tells us that Jesus passed out of sight of his disciples (Luke 24:50–52; Acts 1:9–11). This does not, however, mean that he would have withdrawn further from the spot where the disciples were standing or from the surface of the earth, like a balloon or a spaceship disappearing in a remote distance. On the contrary, the disciples and the first generation of Christians were firmly convinced that after his Ascension their Lord was, though invisible, even nearer to them than he had ever been during his earthly life. Aristophanes, the Greek comedian, had already made clear, in his play *The Clouds* that we cannot reach up to or explore the "heavenly things" by swinging in a high-flying hamper.

The study or the form and function of religious language is a modern achievement. Nevertheless, the biblical writings have been translated throughout the centuries and have been made understandable in a variety of languages. As for the New Testament, the number of languages into which it has been translated in its entirety or in parts exceeds fifteen hundred. It is worth remembering that the translation of the New Testament has been an ongoing process from the time when these writings came into existence. That is a fact which is often forgotten by people who instinctively think that the Word of God has its original and authentic form in precisely the shape or language with which they are familiar.

The Scriptures of the Old Testament were translated into Aramaic as well as into Greek during the centuries preceding the New Testament era. The process of translating the Christian writings started when the gospel tradition, the handing over of the sayings of Jesus and of the accounts of his life and death, was transferred, in its earlier stage and in its oral form, from Aramaic into Greek. The Aramaic substratum of our Gospels disappeared very soon and left only a few traces, single words such as *talitha qoum* ("Little girl, get up" [Mark 5:41]) and *ephphatha* ("Be opened" [Mark 7:34]). Already the synoptic Gospels show, in their Greek form, that the process of translation simultaneously implied a reflection or meditation on the sense of the sayings or of the accounts. Some wordings in our Greek text cannot have had equivalents in the original Aramaic, since Greek is a more differentiated language. The relation between translation and explication in the existing Greek text of the Gospels has not yet been thoroughly examined.

Various periods and areas in the history of the Christian Church have manifested a more intense activity in translating the biblical writings. We can notice a corresponding phenomenon in Judaism in the centuries following upon Alexander the Great, when the Aramaic and Greek translations of the Old Testament were made, the Targums and the Septuagint. Christian translations of the Scriptures were carried out in the early church down to the sixth century and by that time in the Mediterranean world, later on in the time of the Reformation, and then in central and northern Europe, and finally in the nineteenth and twentieth centuries in mission fields. The periods of translation activity have evidently shown a corresponding interest in theological matters. This was the case already when the Targums and the Septuagint came into existence, and this can be seen in the early church and in the time of the Reformation. Whether this is true also of our time will have to be judged in a larger perspective.

A retrospective appraisal of the translations of biblical Scriptures which have been made in the course of time leads to the conclusion that there has been a gradually deepening comprehension of what the process of translation implies, what it means to transfer a text from one language into another. When St. Jerome (c. 345–420), the most outstanding biblical scholar of his time, revised the existing Latin translations of the Bible and produced what became known as the Vulgate, he was not able, in spite of his immense learning, to achieve more than a word-for-word rendering into Latin of the Greek original. Notwithstanding its scholarly qualities, the Vulgate does justice neither to the literary Latin of its time nor to the varieties of style in the original Greek sources. There is a multitude of passages in which it is impossible to find out, because of the so-called mechanical literalism of his translation, how Jerome understood the Greek text he had before him.

Luther (1483–1546) managed to deepen the awareness of what it means to translate a text into a living language. In his treatise "On Interpretation," the German reformer says that a translator should watch the mother in the kitchen, the children in the street, and the men in the marketplace and listen to their characteristic sort of speech. Therefore his translation of the Bible into German can be called the first idiomatic translation of Scripture. Other translators have followed in his footsteps.

In recent times those working on translations of the Bible have been able to profit from the achievements of modern linguistics. Now we know that different languages each have their own characteristic grammatical structures. When translating we must transfer a sentence from the structure proper to the source language to a structure which is suited for the receptor language. When it is said in the Greek text that John the Baptizer "proclaimed a baptism of repentance for the forgiveness of sins" (Mark 1 : 4), this can fittingly be rendered, "He proclaimed the forgiveness of sins through repentance and baptism." Or let us take the narrative of the curing of a blind man at Bethsaida. When Jesus asks him whether he could see anything, the answer is in older translations: "I see men; but they look like trees, walking" (Mark 8 : 24 RSV). This scarcely makes sense and does not do justice either to the Greek text or to the claims to clarity in an English sentence. The proper English equivalent to the Greek is rather: "I can see people. They look like trees, but they are walking about." This rendering places the perceptions of the man who began to see again in the right order; the word *but* comes in the proper place.

A translator should have a good command of the source language as well as the receptor language. But this is not sufficient. Above all he must have reached a thorough understanding of the text that he is dealing with. It can rightly be said that every translation presupposes and implies an appropriate interpretation of the text that is translated. Otherwise the translator will not be able to control the work he is performing, nor will the future reader of the translation arrive at a true and comprehensive understanding of the content and message of the text. During the last two centuries and not least in our own time, the process of interpreting and understanding a text—also apart from the particular problems of a translation—has been made the object of a special field of research, hermeneutics. And *hermeneutics,* a Greek word derived from the name Hermes-Mercurius, the guide among the gods, means precisely the art of interpretation.

The first one to deal with these questions and to use the term *hermeneutics,* which had been created a century earlier, was the German theologian and philosopher F. D. E. Schleiermacher (1768–1834). Trying to elucidate the way that leads to the understanding of a text, he pointed out the importance of the context. And the context of a textual passage to be interpreted, according to his definition, is not only the adjacent parts of the writing in question but in a wider sense the whole setting of the text in its time and in its cultural environment. In his study of the process of interpretation, Schleiermacher also coined the term *hermeneutic circle.* To this metaphor he attributed the following signification: a continually repeated confrontation of a text with its context—context meaning the structure and train of thought in the whole writing in question on one hand and the historical setting of the writing on the other. Each confrontation will give a deepened understanding of both text and context. The metaphor of the hermeneutic circle is not perfectly adequate, though. We should rather call it a spiral, since the repeated confrontations lead to widened views and a fuller understanding.

A few examples may illustrate what the hermeneutic circle means in the sense given to it by Schleiermacher. Leaven is used as an image or as a metaphor in the sayings of Jesus. But strangely enough it has two entirely different meanings. In a parable, the kingdom of God is compared with leaven or yeast which a woman takes and kneads into three measures of flour, which makes the whole mass of dough rise (Matt. 13: 33–34). In a saying Jesus tells his disciples to be on guard against the yeast of the Pharisees and Sadducees (Matt. 16:6). In the parable, leaven has a positive signification—the growth of the kingdom is something eagerly expected. In the saying, the signification is negative, as it is also in Paul's exhortation: "Do you not know that a little yeast affects all the dough. Get rid of the old yeast to make of yourself fresh dough" (1 Cor. 5:6–7). It is in fact the context that determines the signification of the image in the passages in which it appears. Attempts have been made by some biblical students to interpret the leaven in the parable in a negative sense, but there a renewed confrontation of text and context shows that the spreading of the leaven is equivalent in meaning to the growth of the seed. Therefore, the leaven of the parable is a positive image or symbol, whereas the leaven of the Pharisees and Sadducees—that is, their burdensome interpretation of the law—inevitably is a negatively loaded metaphor.

When the church fathers and exegetes in more recent times explained the term *Son of Man* in the sayings of Jesus, they stressed the fact that Jesus was a real man, a human being and not only a divine person. Modern biblical studies have brought about detailed confrontations of the sayings in the Gospel with Old Testament Scriptures and Jewish writings, indeed a repeated hermeneutic circle. In this way it has definitely become clear that the Son of Man is not primarily human but on the contrary a divine figure (cf. Dan. 7:13–14; 1 Enoch 46–49; 61–62; 70–71).

In Psalm 23 older translations read, "Even though I walk in the valley of the shadow of death" (v. 4). Modern research in the vocabulary of the Hebrew language, however (and the Hebrew language is one of the contexts of the psalm) has shown that the words in question in the original text do not mean the valley of the shadow of death but a dark valley. A coherent analysis of the motifs of verses 1 through 4, which are all taken from a shepherd's daily life, confirms this. Thus an interpretative operation as it is described by the hermeneutic circle has made impossible a translation which many readers of the psalms have cherished and will certainly miss. But the context of the passage outranges our personal preferences.

In our own time, the German philosopher and protagonist of existentialism, Martin Heidegger (1889–1976), inaugurated a new phase of hermeneutical reflection, and he was followed by H. G. Gadamer (1900–    ), who made contributions of his own to the study of the process of interpretation. Attention was now focused not only on the text but also on the person of the interpreter. He who interprets a text forms, in another way, part of a context, determined by the time in which he works and by the setting in which he lives. The fact that the interpreter is determined by his context is likely to affect his interpretation of a text.

With Heidegger, the symbol of the hermeneutic circle received its second signification: a continually repeated confrontation of the text (considered in the whole of its context) on one hand and of the interpreter (within his proper context) on the other. Gadamer speaks here of two horizons of interpretation, that of the text and that of the interpreter.

Again, the continued confrontation of the two horizons could be more adequately described not as a circle but as a spiral leading to widened insights.

As an example of the hermeneutic circle in its second signification, we can once again choose the figure of the Son of Man as it appears in the sayings of Jesus. The fact that it was interpreted, in ancient and medieval times, as a name indicating Christ's condition of being human also and not exclusively divine shows that the interpretation was made not on the basis of the text (the sayings of Jesus) and its context (the writings of the New Testament and Daniel 7, for example, in the Old Testament) but out of the need of Christian teaching in times when the manhood of Christ was exposed to doubts. Thus the interest of catechism, which formed part of the context of the interpreters, prejudiced the understanding of a central term in the Gospels.

Another example is furnished by a passage in that chapter of 1 Corinthians in which Paul discusses questions about marriage that had been put to him. In that context he writes, according to older translations (vv. 36–38): "If there is anyone who feels it would not be fair to his daughter to let her grow too old for marriage, and that he should do something about it, he is free to do as he likes: he is not sinning if there is a marriage. On the other hand, if someone has firmly made up his mind, without any compulsion and in complete freedom of choice, to keep his daughter as she is, he will be doing a good thing. In other words, the man who sees that his daughter is married has done a good thing but the man who keeps his daughter unmarried has done something even better" (JB 1966). In a note it is said that in the classical world a father made what arrangements he thought fit for his daughter.

The strange thing is that the Greek original of this passage contains neither the word *father* nor the word *daughter*. The circumstances indicated in the translation above seem odd and unrealistic. And there is no support in the context for an argument like this. In recent times it has become clear that this passage has been completely misunderstood by translators and commentators for more than fifteen hundred years. It is not about a father's concern about arranging a decent marriage for his daughter—far from it. Having previously taught the Christian community at Corinth that each one should stay in the social condition he lived in when the Lord called him, and this in view of the imminent return of

Christ, Paul now answers a question that had been sent from Corinth. Married couples should continue to be married and unmarried men and women should not care to marry. But what about young people who were engaged? There Paul gives the following advice, and here we cite the undoubtedly correct translation of the passage. "If a man feels he is behaving indecently toward his girl because his instinct is too powerful and he has no choice, let him do as he wishes: he commits no sin, let them marry. If the man, however, stands firm in his resolve and if he without constraint is free to carry out his will and has made up his mind to keep his girl untouched, then he acts rightly. To sum up: the man who marries his girl, acts fitly; the one who does not, will do better" (see RSV, NAB).

What has this to do with the hermeneutic circle? The circle in its first signification does not explain the fact that the passage has been misinterpreted for such a long time. There is nothing in the context that suggests the traditional understanding. But the circle in its second signification draws our attention to the fact that the interpreter can be influenced and prejudiced by his own context. Undoubtedly pious readers of St. Paul's letters throughout the ages would have shrunk at the slightest thought that the apostle could have had sexual instincts in his mind and would have discussed them with straightforward words. In this century our own context, the world we live in, has become less prudish and certainly more outspoken, and therefore we can now comprehend Paul's advice in a new, realistic, and certainly more adequate way.

Similar reactions have tinged the translation of a characteristic word in a couple of sayings in the Gospels. When Jesus speaks of hell—for example, "Whoever insults his brother shall be liable to the hell of fire," in a modern translation rather "fire of hell" or "burning hell" (Matt. 5:22)—the Greek text has a wording which in a literal rendering reads "Gehenna of fire" or "burning Gehenna." And Gehenna, in Hebrew gē-hinnōm, the valley of Hinnom, was a ravine at the southern end of Jerusalem. In ancient times a place in this valley was the scene of an idolatrous cult involving the burning of children as sacrificial victims to Moloch (Jer. 7:30–8:3). Later, perhaps because of its bad reputation, the valley became the dumping ground where the refuse of the city was burned. Therefore, Moffatt's translation (1913) and the New American Bible have in their texts of Matthew 5:22 "the fire of Gehenna," whereas Phillips (1958) has "the fire of destruction" in Matthew 5:22 and "rubbish-heap" (garbage dump) in Mark 9:43, 45.

Viewed within the scope of the text and examined according to the directions of the hermeneutic circle in its first significance, these modern renderings are not satisfactory. For by the time of Jesus the word *Gehenna* had evolved from a topographical designation to an eschatological term signifying an everlasting punishment. This development was partly due to influences from other religions, not least Persian. Therefore, the English word *hell* is in fact equivalent to the Greek (or Hebrew) *Gehenna* because this English word expresses the idea of a transcendent punishment.

But in some English translations of the Gospels, why has *hell* been changed to *Gehenna*? Here the hermeneutical circle in its second signification shows its relevance. The context of the translators influenced the interpretation of the text in this case. In modern times the word *hell* was considered too frightening and too definitive, and therefore the whole complex of a final punishment was mercifully obscured by using empty renderings like *Gehenna* or *rubbish heap*.

An ideal translation of the New Testament should allow anyone who reads it to understand the Gospels and the Epistles in the same way as those who wrote these texts in their original form or those who read them when they had just been written. Today's readers of a modern translation of Paul's letter to the Philippians should be in the position to grasp its message in the same way and to the same extent as did the members of the Christian community at Macedonian Philippi when Paul's letter arrived and was read to them about 60 A.D. That goal is certainly utopian, but an ideal to aim at.

In order to facilitate, as far as possible, a comprehension of what Paul wrote some nineteen hundred years ago, it is necessary to supply to a modern reader the information that Christians at ancient Philippi had in their heads. When Paul wrote, "Even if my life is to be poured out as a libation over the sacrificial service of your faith, I am glad of it and rejoice with all of you" (Phil. 2:17), the addressees of his letter would know the pictorial language that the apostle used and would understand what these metaphors meant. They had temples in their city and were familiar with sacrificial rites. A reader in our time needs to be informed about ceremonies in the sanctuaries of the Greco-Roman world.

Such information can suitably be provided in notes at the bottom of a page.

In Protestant tradition it has long been a kind of dogma that Holy Scripture should be accessible to pious readers without notes or comments. Readers of the Bible should not be influenced or become prejudiced. In recent times, however, most translations, irrespective of confessional traditions, are being equipped with notes, the necessity of which is now commonly recognized. I am not sure whether biblical students are aware that the supply of notes in translations of the Bible is a consequence of the insights provided by the hermeneutic circle in its first significance. I do know that the demand for explanations promoting the understanding of the translated text will certainly not cease.

Moreover, necessary information can be put into the very wording of a translation. In Acts 18 : 12 Luke writes about an incident at the time of St. Paul's stay in Corinth. "During Gallio's proconsulship in Achaia, the Jews rose against Paul and brought him before the bench." It is precisely this statement that allows us to date not only Paul's visit to the capital of the Roman province Achaia but, in an approximative way, the whole itinerary of Paul's travels. When the book of Acts was written, every reader of it would have known that a proconsulship lasted one year and thus marks a limited space of time. Therefore the new Swedish translation of the New Testament reads, "in the year when Gallio was proconsul of Achaia," though the words *in the year* are not in the Greek text. Further details about Gallio and about the importance of this dating are given in a note.

In Acts 11:28, when a worldwide famine in the time of the early church is mentioned, the Greek text has, "This happened in the days of Claudius." An ancient reader would have known that Claudius was a Roman emperor and that he reigned from 41 through 54 A.D. The New American Bible therefore has every reason to write, "It did in fact occur while Claudius was emperor," though the word *emperor* is not in the original text.

As yet, no elaborate answer has been given to the question of to what extent modern methods of translation, such as the transformation of grammatical structures in order to provide an idiomatic translation, result from the achievements of hermeneutics in the way that these achievements are illustrated by the hermeneutic circle in its second signification. A translation must transfer the content of the original text from the horizon of that text, its means of expression, to the horizon of the modern reader, to the structures of thought and language that are familiar to him.

Linguistics, a field of studies cultivated in our time, has made clear that the meaning of a sentence is conveyed not by single words placed in a row but by the sentence as a whole, by the sum of its words in their syntactical structure. A word-for-word translation will therefore always remain defective. The elementary units in a text are not words but clauses, sentences, and trains of thought.

Different languages, though, show characteristic differences in their way of structuring sentences. Therefore the reader of a translation will be frustrated—or at least he will not be sufficiently stimulated—in his efforts to understand the text if the translation renders, in a purely mechanical way, the sequences of words as they appear in the original text, and if it does not transfer the structures of the source language to such new structures as are proper to the receiver language. Carrying out an idiomatic translation requires a never-ceasing reconsideration of linguistic structures.

The words *love of God* can mean that God loves us or that we love God. The Greeks had sensitive ears and were able to catch the actual signification of this expression from the context. A German thesis bears the title, "Communion with Christ in the light of Paul's use of the genitive" (O. Schmitz, 1924). Thus a modern translation of Paul's letters will have to make clear, by a change of grammatical structure, the meaning of a Greek genitive where it is not evident. "Love of God" will have to be translated "God's love for us" or "our love for God," provided that the biblical author did not want to leave the matter in suspense.

When Paul writes, "we give thanks to God . . . remembering your work in faith, and labor of love, and patience of hope in our Lord Jesus Christ" (1 Thess. 1 : 2–3), he uses a series of genitive constructions that look awkward to a modern European eye. An idiomatic translation would be, "remembering the way you are proving your faith, and laboring in love, and enduring in your hope of our Lord Jesus Christ."

It can thus be stated in a general way that every translation implies or presupposes an interpretation. Gadamer is right when he maintains (in his masterpiece *Wahrheit und Methode*, 1963) that a text lying before

us in a foreign language offers only somewhat more complicated problems than does a text written in our native language.

In some instances we must deal not only with the text of the New
Testament in its Greek form but also with another text in another source
language behind the text that is the object of translation. So it is whenever quotations from the Old Testament are inserted into the text of the
Gospels, the Epistles, or other writings. People often ask: Can you translate the New Testament before having finished a translation of the Old
Testament? A positive answer to this question can easily be given, since
all quotations from the Old Testament appear in Greek and therefore
had already been translated from their original Hebrew or Aramaic
shape before they were brought into a new context in the writings of the
New Testament.

A problem of interpretation and, as a consequence, of translation appears in two well-known sections of the Gospels—in the narratives of
the announcement of the birth of Jesus in Matthew (chap. 1) and Luke
(chap. 1). Luke contains the scene in which the angel Gabriel is sent to a
young woman betrothed to a man named Joseph, of the house of David;
her name was Mary. She was, according to the rules observed by that
time, some twelve or thirteen years old (v. 26f). Now the Greek word
*parthenos,* which is used twice in this passage, can mean both "girl"
(which is the usual sense in the Greek language from old times) and
"virgin" (for example, used in reference to the patroness of classical
Athens, Virgin Athena). Sometimes it can also mean unmarried women
who are not virgins. All depends upon the context.

When the narrative starts, Luke has not told his readers that Mary is
a virgin in the special sense of the English word. This aspect does not
come in until Mary replies to the announcement of the angel that she
will bear a son, saying, "How can this be since I have never had a hus-
band?" (v.34).

The traditional translation *virgin* in the beginning of the narrative is
not motivated by the context but is the result of Christian understanding and teaching. When Luke wrote the narrative, he obviously knew
about the virginity of Mary. But if he had wanted his reader to understand, from the beginning of the paragraph, the word *parthenos* in the
special sense of "virgin," he could have made this clear by adding an
adjective such as *chaste,* as St. Paul does when he speaks of himself as

presenting the Christian community at Corinth as a chaste virgin to Christ (2 Cor. 11:2). Therefore it is appropriate to translate the opening sentence of the narrative in the following way. "The angel Gabriel was sent from God to a young girl betrothed to a man named Joseph . . . and the girl's name was Mary." That is what the text says to anyone who reads it with fresh eyes. In verse 34 the reader will learn that the girl was a virgin.

Further complications turn up in the parallel section in Matthew. There the announcement of the birth of Jesus is addressed to Joseph. The angel of the Lord appears to him in a dream and tells him to take Mary as his wife. By Holy Spirit she has conceived a child and is to have a son. Then the evangelist states, "All this happened to fulfil what the Lord had said through the prophet: 'The virgin shall be with child and give birth to a son, and they shall call him Emmanuel'" (Matt. 1:22f).

The prophet quoted here is Isaiah, and the Greek text of the quotation has the word *parthenos,* here translated "virgin." Is this translation correct, and what is the meaning of the passage in the original Hebrew text?

The book of Isaiah, chapter 7, tells us that Ahaz, the king of Judah, is severely threatened by his adversaries in the north, the kingdoms of Israel and of Aram, during the Syro-Ephraemitic war of 735–733 B.C. The Lord gives him a sign in the form of an oracle. "The young woman shall be with child, and bear a son, and shall name him Immanuel" (7:14). The solemn oracle is spoken in a situation when the royal family feared that the Davidic dynasty might be overthrown and the promise made to David's house cancelled. The child about to be born may be the future king Hezekiah, whose mother would have been, by the time the oracle was pronounced, a young unmarried woman. Later on, the solemnity of the oracle and the name Immanuel lead to the opinion that the oracle's perspective did not confine itself to the birth of Hezekiah. The promise made to Ahaz was believed to announce the birth of an ideal king of David's line through whose coming the messianic era would be inaugurated.

Now Isaiah, in the oracle given to Ahaz, does not use the technical term in Hebrew for "virgin" (*betūlā*) but a word that denotes a young woman, whether married or not (*'almā*). It is certainly not evident that Isaiah, when inserting the promise of the birth of a royal child into his account of a series of oracles addressed to king Ahaz, took into consideration the possibility of a virgin conceiving a child. Traditional Christian interpretation, however, makes Isaiah in his time proclaim not a happy event in the royal family of Ahaz some 700 years B.C., but the birth of the Messiah from a virgin, a unique event at the beginning of a new age. An immense literature has grown up around this passage, and the meaning of the Hebrew 'almā—young woman or virgin—as well as the perspective of the promise is incessantly discussed. The New American Bible still reads "virgin" in its translation of Isaiah 7 : 14.

Perhaps the most interesting point is the translation of the book of Isaiah in the Greek Septuagint, carried out in the centuries preceding the time of Christ. There the Hebrew 'almā has been rendered by *parthenos*, which in this context probably means precisely "virgin." It looks as if the idea that the Messiah would be born of a virgin had originated in Hellenistic Judaism, presumably in Egyptian Alexandria, where the Septuagint translation was made. Contrary to what has often been maintained, the idea of the birth of a divine Savior of a virgin, in the strict sense of the word, has no veritable analogy in any other religion.

Now we can go back to Matthew (1 : 23), where we started a while ago. Does the Greek word *parthenos*, in the Gospel's quotation from Isaiah (7 : 14) mean "young woman" or "virgin"? As Matthew quotes the Septuagint and as the Septuagint apparently had adopted the idea in its translation of Isaiah 7 : 14 that the Messiah would be born of a virgin, *parthenos* in Matthew 1 : 23 must signify a virgin in the proper sense of the word. This signification is confirmed by the context in Matthew's narrative of the birth of Jesus. With the help of a quotation from Scripture the evangelist wants to prove that the miraculous way in which Mary is going to have a son is consistent with the divine plan of salvation, intimated in the writings of the Prophets.

Is Christian belief getting poorer if we relinquish the conviction that Isaiah, already in the eighth century B.C. and in a clearly apprehended manner, predicted the birth of the future Messiah of a virgin? Quite the contrary. The mystery that is proclaimed in Scripture is deepened in its dimensions if we allow for a development in Jewish thought from the era of the kingdom down to Hellenistic times. The idea of the virgin birth was not static, inspired from above and passively received by the prophet. It was rather conceived and successively elaborated—because it was thought to be essential—in the period between the return from the exile (539 B.C.) and the completion of the Septuagint (second century B.C.). A first-rate Jewish scholar who shares this opinion is David Flusser of the University of Jerusalem.

No translator should fail to acquaint himself with the theories about translating that are based upon the generative transformation grammar, a model in modern linguistics launched by Dr. Noam Chomsky (1928–   ) of the Massachusetts Institute of Technology. Dr. Chomsky's ideas have been stimulating in different fields of linguistic research but have also been severely criticized. In order to facilitate the heavy work of Bible translators toiling in different countries and with numbers of languages, generative grammar has been systematized and made a practical tool by Dr. Eugene Nida and his collaborators in the United Bible Societies (*Toward a Science of Translation,* 1964, and *The Theory and Practice of Translation,* 1969).

Without entering into the problem of whether translating is a craft or a creative work—there are endless discussions of this question—we can notice that serious attempts are made to convert translating into a rational technique. The essential procedure of this technique is to reduce sentences in the original text, usually called source text, into "kernels." This step is called back-transformation. A passage from Ephesians 1:7 can offer an example. The reduction into kernels implies a logical analysis that aims at making clear the logical subject in every single part of the original sentence. The Authorized Version, which is quoted by Dr. Nida, reads this passage as follows. "In him [Christ] we have redemption through his blood, the forgiveness of our trespasses, according to the riches of his grace which he lavished upon us."

With the help of generative transformation the sentence is analyzed and transformed into five kernels, in which the logical subjects of the different grammatical elements in the sentence are clearly indicated:
1. God redeems us.
2. Christ dies (sheds his blood).
3. God forgives.
4. We sin.
5. God shows grace richly.

Having been formulated, the kernels can be translated into the receptor language. It is easier to translate uncomplicated kernels than an elaborate sentence in the original text.

Finally the kernels, in their new shape in the receptor language, have to be restructured into sentences which do justice to that language, and by this step in the procedure a readable text in the receptor language is established. This restructuring to a new surface structure can be carried out independently of the surface structure of the original text.

A rapid comparison of the kernels with the original sentence shows that interrelations between the five kernels are lacking. In ordinary speech the interrelations of different elements of thought are expressed by grammatical structures. The kernels do not tell us why or in what way God shows grace richly. In the original sentence we learn without difficulty that God shows grace when he redeems us by forgiving our sins through the suffering and death of Christ. This chain of thought must not be lost in the course of translation.

A critical examination of this technique leads to unexpected surprises. First, back-transformation, the reduction of a sentence into kernels, can reasonably be carried out only in the native language of the translator. Which translator would be able to formulate kernels in Greek, not to speak of Hebrew? In the handbooks referred to above, the source text is not the Greek New Testament but the Authorized Version. But neither the Authorized Version nor any other version of the Bible can ever replace the original Greek or Hebrew text.

Second, because of their simplicity, the kernels are unable to do justice to the complicated structure, not only of grammar but of thought, in an original sentence. Reduction into kernels will inevitably imply a reduction of content, an impoverishment of the text.

And third, every translation must be preceded by and based on an interpretation of the text that is translated. Both handbooks and commentaries in which the method of generative grammar is applied show that the procedure of back-transformation, transfer, and restructuring are mechanical to the extent that they block all possibilities to arrive at a delicate and sensitive understanding of the text. Earlier interpretations are reproduced in an uncritical way. Transformative analysis does not lead the translator to a creative confrontation with the text but makes him a slave of other translations and of superficial commentaries.

The method of translating by means of generative transformation grammar has been conceived with the intention to make translating a rational and, in the last resort, quantitative operation. One underlying assumption is that when different translators have analyzed the same text, they will have arrived at the same number of kernels and will have formulated them in exactly the same way. In this way the process of translation will be withdrawn from the arbitrariness of the translators. And if this is possible, it will also be possible to entrust the whole work to a computer. But only those data can be quantified and put into a computer that are known to us beforehand. A computer is able to work up a maximum of information in a minimum of time. However, we ought to realize that this machine—as are all machines—is stupid. It can never achieve anything (output) which has not, on principle and in elements, been fed into it (input).

Translating, in the true sense of the word, is not a quantitative but a qualitative operation. This can be illustrated by the hermeneutic circle in its second signification: the ongoing confrontation of text and translator within their horizons. When working with his translation, the translator continually discovers new aspects, is challenged to make new decisions, and reaches new solutions. He stands in a dialectic tension between faithfulness and unfaithfulness: he has to be utmost faithful to his text and critically unfaithful to preconceived and prejudiced opinions about the text—opinions of his own or those taken over from others. That makes translation an art.

# Jesus the Jew*

GEZA VERMES

"JESUS THE JEW" is an emotionally charged synonym for the Jesus of history, as opposed to the divine Christ, that simply restates the fact— still hard for many Christians and even some Jews to accept—that Jesus was a Jew and not a Christian. It implies a renewed quest for the historical figure reputed to be the founder of Christianity.

The search is surprising in one respect: namely, that it has been undertaken at all. In another, it is unusual in that it has been made without any ulterior motive. My intention has been to reach for the historical truth for the sake of putting the record straight, but definitely not in order to demonstrate some theological preconception.

If in continuity with medieval Jewish tradition I had set out to prove that Jesus was not only a false Messiah, but also a heretic and a sorcerer, my research would have been prejudiced from the start. Even if I had chosen as my target the more trendy effort of yesterday, the repatriation of Jesus into the Jewish people, it is unlikely to have led to an untendentious inquiry, to an analysis of the available evidence without fear or

---

* This is a revised version of the 1974 C. G. Montefiore lecture. For its final version, see *Jesus and the World of Judaism* (SCM Press, London, 1983, and Fortress Press, Philadelphia, 1984), 1–14.

favor. By the same token, when a committed Christian embarks on such a task with a mind already persuaded by the dogmatic suppositions of his church, which postulate that Jesus was not only the true Messiah, but the only begotten Son of God—that is to say, God himself—he is bound to attribute the maximum possible Christian traditional significance even to the most neutral sentence, one that in any other context he would not even be tempted to interpret that way.

My purpose has been to look into the past for some trace of the features of the first-century Galilean before he had been proclaimed either the Second Person of the Holy Trinity or the apostate and bogeyman of Jewish popular thought. Strangely enough, because of the special nature of the Gospels, a large group of Christians, including such opposing factions as the out-and-out fundamentalists and the highly sophisticated New Testament critics, would consider a historical inquiry of this sort necessarily doomed to failure. Our knowledge of Jesus, they would claim, depends solely on the New Testament: writings that were never intended as history but as the experience of the faith of Jesus's first followers. The fundamentalists deduce from these premises that the truth embedded in the Gospels is accessible only to those who share the evangelists' outlook. Those who do not are, to quote a letter published in an English newspaper "still in the night . . . and so [have] no title to write about things which are only known to believers."

At the other extreme stand some of the leading spokesmen of contemporary New Testament scholarship. Instead of asserting with the fundamentalists that no quest for the historical Jesus should be attempted, they are firmly convinced that no such quest can be initiated. "I do indeed think," writes Rudolf Bultmann (1962, 14), "that we can know now almost nothing concerning the life and personality of Jesus, since the early Christian sources show no interest in either."

Against both these viewpoints, and against Christian and Jewish denominational bias, I seek to reassert the inalienable right of the historian to pursue a course independent of beliefs. Yet, I will at the same time try to indicate that, despite widespread academic skepticism, our considerably increased knowledge of the Palestinian-Jewish realities of the time of Jesus enables us to extract historically reliable information even from nonhistorical sources such as the Gospels. In fact, with the discovery and study of the Dead Sea Scrolls and other archaeological treasures, and the corresponding improvement in our understanding of the languages and culture of the Jews of New Testament times, it is now possible not only to place Jesus in relief against this setting, as students of the Jewish background of Christianity pride themselves on doing, but to insert him legitimately within first-century Jewish life itself. The questions then to be asked are where he fits into it, and whether the added substance and clarity gained from immersing him in historical reality confers credibility on the patchy Gospel picture.

Let us begin then by selecting a few noncontroversial facts concerning Jesus's life and activity and endeavor to build on these foundations. Jesus lived in Galilee, a province governed during his lifetime not by the Romans, but by a son of Herod the Great. His hometown was Nazareth, an insignificant place not referred to by Josephus, the Mishnah, or the Talmud, and first mentioned outside the New Testament and Christian sources in an inscription from the Palestinian coastal city of Caesarea, dating to the third or fourth century. Whether he was born there, or somewhere else, is uncertain. The Bethlehem legend is in any case highly suspect.

As for the date of his birth, this "is not truly a historical problem," writes one of the greatest living experts on antiquity, Sir Ronald Syme (1973) despite the many efforts deployed to establish it since the second century to the present day, counting years forward and backward, rereading, reinterpreting, or misinterpreting inscriptions and documents. The year of Jesus's death is also absent from the sources. Nevertheless the general chronological context is clearly defined. He was crucified under Pontius Pilate, the prefect of Judaea from 26 to 36 C.E.; his public ministry is said to have taken place shortly after the fifteenth year of Tiberius (28/29 C.E.), when John the Baptist inaugurated his mission of repentance. Whether Jesus taught for one, two, or three years, his execution in Jerusalem must have occurred in the early thirties of the first century.

He was fairly young when he died. Luke (3:23) reports that he was approximately thirty years old when he joined John the Baptist. Also one of the few points on which Matthew and Luke, the only two evangelists to elaborate on the events preceding and following Jesus's birth, agree is in dating those events to the days of King Herod of Judaea, who died in the spring of 4 B.C.E. (Matt. 2:1–16; Luke 1:5).

Let me try to sketch the world of Jesus in the second and third decades of the first century. In distant Rome, Tiberius reigned supreme. Valerius Gratus and Pontius Pilate were governing Judaea. Joseph Caiaphas was high priest of the Jews, the president of the Jerusalem Sanhedrin, and the head of the Sadducees. Hillel and Shammai, the leaders of the most influential Pharisaic schools, were possibly still alive, and during the lifetime of Jesus, Gamaliel the Elder became Hillel's successor. Not far from Jerusalem, a few miles south of Jericho on the shore of the Dead Sea, the ascetic Essenes were worshipping God in holy withdrawal and planning the conversion of the rest of Jewry to the true Judaism known only to them, the followers of the Teacher of Righteousness. And in neighboring Egypt, in Alexandria, the philosopher Philo was busy harmonizing the Jewish life-style with the wisdom of Greece, a dream cherished by the civilized Jews of the Diaspora.

In Galilee, the quasi independence of which depended entirely on imperial favor, the tetrarch Herod Antipas remained lord of life and death and continued to hope (in vain) that one day the emperor might end his humiliation by granting him the title of king. At the same time, following the upheaval that accompanied the tax registration ordered in 6 C.E. by the legate of Syria, Publius Sulpicius Quirinius, Judas the Galilean and his sons were stimulating the revolutionary tendencies of the uncouth northerners, tendencies which had resulted in the foundation of the Zealot movement.

Such was the general ambiance in which the personality and character of Jesus the Jew were formed. We know nothing concrete, however, about his education and training, his contacts, or the influences to which he may have been subjected; for quite apart from the unhistorical nature of the stories relating to his infancy and childhood, the interval between his twelfth year and the start of his public ministry is wrapped in total silence by all four evangelists. Jesus spent not only his early years, but also the greatest part of his public life in Galilee. If we adopt the chronology of the synoptic Gospels (Matthew, Mark, and Luke) with their one-year ministry, apart from brief excursions to Phoenicia (now Lebanon) and Perea (present-day Golan Heights or northern Transjordan), he left his province only once, for the fateful journey to Jerusalem at Passover. But even if the longer timetable of John's Gospel is followed, the Judean stays of Jesus corresponded to the mandatory pilgrimages to the Temple, and as such were of short duration. Therefore, if we are to understand him, it is into the Galilean world that we must look.

The Galilee of Jesus, especially his own part of it, Lower Galilee around the Lake of Gennesaret, was a rich and mostly agricultural country. The inhabitants were proud of their independence and jealous of their Jewishness, in which regard, despite doubts often expressed by Judeans, they considered themselves second to none. They were also brave and tough. Josephus, the commander-in-chief of the region during the first Jewish War, praises their courage and describes them as people "from infancy inured to war" (*Jewish War* 3, 41).

In effect, in the mountains of Upper Galilee rebellion against the government, any government—Hasmonean, Herodian, Roman—was endemic between the middle of the first century B.C.E. and 70 C.E. from Ezekias, the *archilēstēs* (the chief brigand or revolutionary) whose uprising was put down by young Herod, through the arch-Zealot Judas the Galilean and his rebellious sons, to John the son of Levi from Gush Halav and his "Galilean contingent," notorious in besieged Jerusalem for their "mischievous ingenuity and audacity" at the time of the 66–70 C.E. war (*Jewish War* 4, 558). In short, the Galileans were admired as staunch fighters by those who sympathized with their rebellious aims; those who did not thought of them as dangerous hotheads.

In Jerusalem and in Judean circles they had also the reputation of being an unsophisticated people. In rabbinic parlance, a Galilean is usually referred to as *Gelili shoteh*, stupid Galilean. He is presented as a typical peasant, a boor, an *'am ha-aretz* (a religiously uneducated person). Cut off from the Temple and the study centers of Jerusalem, Galilean popular religion appears to have depended not so much on the authority of the priests or on the scholarship of scribes as on the magnetism of their local saints like Jesus's younger contemporary, Hanina ben Dosa, the celebrated miracle worker.

These lengthy preliminaries done with, it is time now to turn to the Gospels to make our acquaintance with Jesus the Jew, or more exactly, Jesus the *Galilean* Jew. I intend to leave to one side the speculations of the early Christians concerning the various divinely contrived roles of Messiah, Lord, Son of God, and so on, that their Master was believed to have fulfilled before or after his death. Instead, I will rely on those simple and largely undistorted accounts of the first three Gospels which suggest that Jesus impressed his countrymen, and acquired fame among them, chiefly as a charismatic teacher, healer, and exorcist. However, my purpose is not to discuss his teaching. Few will contest that his message was essentially Jewish, or that on certain controversial issues (for example, whether the dead would rise again) he voiced the opinion of the Pharisees.

His renown, the evangelists proclaim, had spread throughout Galilee. According to Mark, when Jesus and his disciples disembarked from their boat on Lake Kinneret of Tiberias, "he was immediately recognized; and the people scoured the whole country-side and brought the sick on stretchers to any place where he was reported to be. Wherever he went, to farmsteads, villages or towns, they laid out the sick in the market places and begged him to let them simply touch the edge of his cloak; and all who touched him were cured" (Mark 6 : 54−56). Similarly, referring to events in Capernaum, Mark writes: "They brought to him all who were ill and possessed by devils. . . . He healed many who suffered from various diseases, and drove out many devils" (Mark 1 : 33−34). And both Luke and Mark report Jesus himself as saying, "Today and tomorrow, I shall be casting out devils and working cures" (Luke 13 : 32). And, "It is not the healthy that need a doctor but the sick; I did not come to invite virtuous people but sinners" (Mark 2 : 17).

To assess correctly Jesus's healing and exorcistic activities, it is necessary to know that in bygone ages the Jews understood that a relationship existed between sickness, the devil, and sin. As a logical counterpart to such a concept of ill health, it was believed until as late as the third century B.C.E. that recourse to the services of a physician demonstrated a lack of faith, since healing was a monopoly of God. The only intermediaries thought licit between God and the sick were men of God, such as the prophets Elijah and Elisha. By the beginning of the second pre-Christian century, however, the physician's office was made more or less respectable by the requirement that he, too, should be personally holy. The Wisdom writer, Jesus ben Sira, advised the devout when sick to pray, repent, and send gifts to the Temple, and subsequently to call in the physician, who would ask God for insight into the cause of the sickness and for the treatment needed to remedy it. As Ecclesiasticus words it, "The Lord has imparted knowledge to men that by the use of His marvels He may win praise; by employing them, the doctor relieves pain" (Ecclus. 38:6–7).

Jesus's healing gifts are never attributed to the study of physical or mental disease, or to any acquired knowledge of cures, but to mysterious power that emanated from him and was transmitted to the sick by contact with his person, or even with his clothes. In the episode of the crippled woman who was bent double and unable to hold herself upright, we read that "He laid his hands on her, and at once she straightened up and began to praise God" (Luke 13:13). Sometimes touch and command went together. A deaf-mute was cured when Jesus placed his own saliva on the sufferer's tongue and ordered his ears to unblock, saying, "Ephphetha: Be opened!" (Mark 7:33–34).

There is, nevertheless, one story in which Jesus performs a cure without being anywhere within sight, let alone within touching distance, of the sick man. Matthew's account of the episode reads:

> When [Jesus] had entered Capernaum a centurion came up to ask his help.
> Sir—he said—a boy of mine lies at home paralyzed. . . .
> Jesus said, I will come and cure him.
> Sir,—replied the centurion—who am I to have you under my roof? You need only say a word and the boy will be cured. I know, for I am myself under orders, with soldiers under me. I say to one, Go!, and he goes; to another, Come here!, and he comes; and to my servant, Do this!, and he does it.
> Jesus heard him with astonishment, and said to the people following him,
> I tell you this: nowhere, even in Israel, have I found such a faith.
> Then he said to the centurion,
> Go home now. Because of your faith, so let it be. At that moment the boy recovered. (Matt. 8:5–13)

I quote this in full not only because of its intrinsic interest, but also in order to compare it with a Talmudic report concerning one of the famous deeds of Jesus's compatriot, Hanina ben Dosa. It will be seen from the second story how closely the two tales coincide.

> It happened that when Rabban Gamaliel's son fell ill, he sent two of his pupils to R. Hanina ben Dosa that he might pray for him. When he saw

them, he went to the upper room and prayed. When he came down, he
said to them,

Go, for the fever has left him.

They said to him,

Are you a prophet?

He said to them,

I am no prophet, neither am I a prophet's son, but this is how I am
blessed: If my prayer is fluent in my mouth, I know that the sick man is
favoured; if not, I know that his disease is fatal.

They sat down, wrote and noted the hour. When they came to Rabban
Gamaliel, he said to them,

By heaven! You have neither detracted from it, nor added to it, but this
is how it happened. It was at that hour that the fever left him and he asked
us for water to drink. (Babylonian Talmud, Berakhoth 34b)

Instead of ascribing physical and mental illness to natural causes,
Jesus's contemporaries saw the former as a divine punishment for sin
instigated by the devil, and the latter as resulting from a direct demonic
possession. Therefore, by controlling these evil spirits, the exorcist was
believed to be acting as God's agent in the work of liberation, healing,
and pardon.

Jesus was an exorcist, but not a professional one: he did not use in-
cantations such as those apparently composed by king Solomon (*Jewish
Antiquities* 8, 45), or foul-smelling substances intolerable even to the
most firmly ensconced of demons. He did not go in for producing
smoke, as young Tobit did, by burning the heart and the liver of a fish
(Tobit 8:2), or for holding under the noses of the possessed the Solo-
monic *baaras* root, the stink of which, so Josephus assures us, drew the
demon out through the nostrils (*Jewish Antiquities* 8, 46–47). Instead,
Jesus confronted with great authority and dignity the demoniacs (luna-
tics, epileptics, and the like) and commanded the devil to depart. This
act is usually said to have been followed by relief, and at least a temporary remission of the symptoms (Matt. 12:34–44). Even in the Gospels, the demons seem to have had an uncanny facility for finding their
way back to their former habitats.

In Mark 5:1–15 we read that Jesus and his disciples

came to the other side of the lake, into the country of the Gerasenes. As he
stepped ashore, a man possessed by an unclean spirit came up to him

from among the tombs where he had his dwelling. He could no longer be controlled; even chains were useless; he had often been fettered and chained up, but he had snapped his chains and broken the fetters. No one was strong enough to master him. And so, unceasingly, night and day, he would cry aloud among the tombs and on the hill-sides and cut himself with stones. When he saw Jesus in the distance, he ran and flung himself down before him, shouting loudly,

. . . In God's name, do not torment me!

For Jesus was already saying to him,

Out, unclean spirit, come out of this man!

. . . The people . . . came to Jesus and saw the madman who had been possessed . . . sitting there clothed and in his right mind; and they were afraid.

Once more I must parallel the Gospel narrative with one concerning Hanina ben Dosa and his encounter with the queen of the demons.

Let no man go out alone at night . . . for Agrath daughter of Mahlath and eighteen myriads of destroying angels are on the prowl, and each of them is empowered to strike. . . . Once she met Hanina ben Dosa and said to him,

Had there been no commendation from heaven, "Take heed of Hanina ben Dosa . . .", I would have harmed you.

He said to her,

Since I am so highly esteemed in heaven, I decree that you shall never again pass through an inhabited place. (Babylonian Talmud, Pesahim 112b)

Jesus, curing the sick and overpowering the forces of evil with the immediacy and simplicity of the Galilean holy man, was seen as a dispenser of health, one of the greatest blessings expected at the end of time, when "the blind men's eyes shall be opened and the ears of the deaf unstopped"; when "the lame man shall leap like a deer, and the tongue of the dumb shout aloud" (Isa. 35:5–6).

But in this chain of cause and effect linking sickness to the devil, one more element remains—sin. Besides healing the flesh and exorcising the mind, the holy man had one other task to perform: the forgiveness of sin. Here I recount the famous story of the paralytic brought to Jesus in Capernaum.

Four men were carrying him, but because of the crowd they could not get near him. So they opened up the roof over the place where Jesus was . . . and they lowered the stretcher on which the paralysed man was lying. When Jesus saw their faith, he said to the paralysed man,

My son, your sins are forgiven. Now there were some lawyers sitting there and they thought to themselves,

Why does the fellow talk like this? This is blasphemy! Who but God alone can forgive sins? Jesus knew in his own mind that this was what they were thinking, and said to them,

Why do you harbour thoughts like these? Is it easier to say to this paralysed man, 'Your sins are forgiven', or to say, 'Stand up, take your bed and walk'? But to convince you that the son of man has right on earth to forgive sins—he turned to the paralysed man—

I say to you, stand up, take your bed and go home! And he got up, and at once took his stretcher and went out in full view of them all. (Mark 2:3–12)

"My son, your sins are forgiven" is of course not the language of experts in the law, but neither is it blasphemy. On the contrary, absolution from the guilt of wrongdoing appears to have been part and parcel of the charismatic style; this is well illustrated in an important Dead Sea Scrolls fragment, the Prayer of Nabonidus, which depicts a Jewish exorcist as having pardoned the Babylonian king's sins, thus curing him of his seven years' illness. In the somewhat elastic but extraordinarily perceptive religious terminology of Jesus and the spiritual men of his age, *to heal, to expel demons,* and *to forgive sins* were interchangeable synonyms. Indeed, the language and behavior of Jesus is reminiscent of holy men of ages even earlier than his own, and it need cause little surprise to read in Matthew that he was known as "the prophet Jesus from Nazareth in Galilee" (Matt. 21:11), and that his Galilean admirers believed he might be one of the biblical prophets, Jeremiah or *Elijah redivivus* (Matt. 16:14). It could be advanced that if he modeled himself on anyone at all it was precisely on Elijah and Elisha, as the following argument with the people of Nazareth would seem to bear out.

Jesus said,

No doubt you will quote the proverb to me, "Physician, heal yourself!" and say, "We have heard of all your doings in Capernaum; do the same here, in your own home town." I tell you this—he went on—no prophet is recognized in his own country. There were many widows in Israel, you may be sure, in Elijah's time . . . yet it was none of these that Elijah was sent, but to a widow at Sarepta in the territory of Sidon. Again in the time of the prophet Elisha there were many lepers in Israel, and not one of them was healed, but only Naaman, the Syrian. (Luke 4 : 23 – 26)

Jesus was a Galilean Hasid: there lies his greatness and also the germ of his tragedy. That he had his share of the notorious Galilean chauvinism would seem clear from the xenophobic statements attributed to him. As one review of my *Jesus the Jew* puts it, "Once he called us 'dogs' and 'swine' and he forbade the Twelve to proclaim the gospel to Gentiles" (*Financial Times* 7 Feb. 1974). But Jesus was also, and above all, an exemplary representative of the fresh and simple religiousness for which the Palestinian north was noted.

And it was in the following respects that he cannot have been greatly loved by the Pharisees: in his lack of expertise and perhaps even interest in legal matters, common to Galileans in general; in his tolerance of deliberate neglect in regard to certain traditional, though not biblical, customs by his followers; in his table fellowship with publicans and whores; and last but not least, in the spiritual authority explicitly or implicitly presumed to underpin his charismatic activities, an authority impossible to check, unlike teachings handed down from master to disciple. Not that there appears to have been any fundamental disagreement between Jesus and the Pharisees on any basic issue, but whereas Jesus, the preacher of repentance, felt free rhetorically to overemphasize the ethical as compared with the ritual—like certain of the prophets before him—he perhaps could be criticized for not paying enough attention to those needs of society which are met by organized religion. As a matter of fact, the Pharisaic insistence on the necessity of faithfulness toward religious observances as well as of a high standard of ethics has been vindicated by Christian moral theology and canon law, evolved over the centuries, that are scarcely less detailed and casuistical than our elaborate Rabbinic-Talmudic legislation!

Nevertheless, the conflict between Jesus of Galilee and the Pharisees of his time would, in normal circumstances, merely have resembled the infighting of factions belonging to the same religious body, like that between Karaites and Rabbanites in the Middle Ages, or between the orthodox and progressive branches of Judaism in modern times. But in the first century circumstances were not normal. An eschatological and politico-religious fever was always close to the point of eruption, if it had not already exploded, and Galilee was a hotbed of nationalist ferment. Incidentally, there is no evidence in my reading of the Gospels that would point to any particular involvement by Jesus in the revolutionary affairs of the Zealots, though it is likely that some of his followers may have been committed rebels and longed to proclaim him as King Messiah destined to liberate his oppressed nation.

But for the representatives of the establishment—Herod Antipas in Galilee and the chief priests and their council in Jerusalem—the prime unenviable task was to maintain law and order and thus avert a major catastrophe. In their eyes, any activity even remotely resembling revolutionary propaganda was not only against the law of the Roman provincial administration, but also murderously foolish, contrary to the national interest, and likely to expose to the vengeance of the invincible emperor not only those actively implicated, but countless thousands of their innocent compatriots. They had to be silenced one way or another, by persuasion or by force, before it was too late. As the high priest is reported to have said of Jesus—and it is immaterial whether he did so or not—"It is more to your interest that one man should die for the people, than that the whole nation should be destroyed" (John 11:50). Such indeed must have been the attitude of the establishment. Not only actual but even potential leadership of a revolutionary movement called for alertness and vigilance. John the Baptist, who according to Josephus was "a good man" and "exhorted the Jews to live righteous lives," became suspect in Herod's eyes because of an eloquence which might "lead to some form of sedition. . . . Herod decided therefore that it would be much better to strike first and be rid of him before his work led to an uprising" (*Jewish Antiquities* 18, 117–18). Jesus, I believe, was the victim of a similar preventive measure devised by the Saducean rulers in the general interest of keeping the peace.

As Jesus was dying on a Roman cross, under a *titulus* which read, "Jesus of Nazareth, king of the Jews," he cried out with a loud voice, "My God, my God, why hast thou forsaken me?" (Mark 15:34). Nothing epitomizes more sharply the tragedy of Jesus the Jew, misunderstood by friend and foe alike, than this despairing cry from the cross. Nor was this the end of it. For throughout the centuries, as age followed age, Christians and Jews allowed it to continue and worsen. His adherents transformed this lover and worshipper of his Father in heaven into an object of worship; and his own people, under the pressures of persecution at the hands of those adherents, mistakenly attributed to Jesus Christian beliefs and dogmas, many of which would have filled this devout Galilean with profound grief and astonishment.

As I have already said, I began my search for the Jesus of history for its own sake, to prove that by employing the right methods something of the authentic image of the Master from Galilee can be recovered from the dark historical past. To my surprise and pleasure, however, at least one of my readers feels that the work may have some interesting side effects. It has been said of *Jesus the Jew* by an anonymous reviewer in the *Times Literary Supplement* (7 Dec. 1973) that it "poses a challenge to Christianity, though it may not be its primary purpose, or intended at all. The implied challenge is that, if Christians wish to return to the historical Jesus, they must also return, in some measure, to the Judaism in which he lived and moved and had his being."

Rather less sure but still encouraging, David Daube, an influential Jewish voice on this subject, after assessing the book's contribution to the quest for the historical framework of Jesus's activity and for his own concept of his vocation, goes on. "Whether it will do much towards removing ill-will and distrust may be doubted. These attitudes are largely independent of scholarly data. Still with luck, it may do a little. The present climate gives some ground for hope." On the Christian side the echoes have been varied. A well-known English Jesuit, Father Thomas Corbishley, describes *Jesus the Jew* as overcrowded, and its learning as oppressive. And one of his less prominent brethren finds, rather depressingly, that "this learned but tedious book" is a "disappointment." However, in general, Christian academic opinion has been sympathetic, yet not wholly convinced. As Professor A. R. C. Leaney (1974) has put it in Oxford's own *Journal of Theological Studies*, "The result is a valuable contribution to scholarship, but it is hard to assess exactly how successful it is."

## Literature Cited

Bultmann, Rudolf. *Jesus and the Word.* Fontana, 1962.

Corbishley, Thomas. *The Tablet,* 8 Dec. 1973, 1179.

Daube, David. *Journal of Jewish Studies* 25 (1974): 336.

Leaney, A. R. C. *Journal of Theological Studies* 25 (1974): 489.

Vermes, Geza. *Jesus the Jew. A Historian's Reading of the Gospels.* Collins, London, 1973; Fortress, Philadelphia, 1981.

Syme, Ronald. "The Titulus Tiburtinus." *Vestigia* 17 (1973): 600.

# Jesus and Christianity*

GEZA VERMES

"WE ARE SO ACCUSTOMED, and rightly, to make Jesus the object of religion that we become apt to forget that in our earliest records he is portrayed not as the object of religion, but as a religious man." Those are not my words. They were written by the renowned New Testament scholar, Thomas Walter Manson (1935, 101). But I could not have found a more fitting quotation. While giving it his approval as a Christian, Manson suddenly understood that the church's general approach to Christ contains an ingredient that conflicts with the best historical evidence. My intention is to explore the Gospels for that evidence, and to piece it together so that we can rediscern the character of Jesus the religious man, and subsequently contrast the essentials of his piety with the main spiritual thrust of the religion of which he has become the object. But first we shall have to inquire into the general religious climate of his place and time in order to view his particular contribution to it in perspective.

In this larger setting, the notion of divine sovereignty, the "yoke of the

* This is a revision of the final Riddell Memorial Lecture delivered at Newcastle University in 1981. For its final version, see *Jesus and the World of Judaism* (SCM Press, London, 1983, and Fortress Press, Philadelphia, 1984), 46–57.

Kingdom," was associated and even interchangeable with the "yoke of the Law," the Torah. Known in the Hebrew Bible as the Law of God or the Law of Moses, it regulated every aspect of private and public existence—agriculture, trading and commerce, the choice and preparation of food, the intimacies of sexuality, and even occasionally the materials and styles of Jewish clothing. As a law-abiding person, Jesus may be presumed to have behaved in respect of these general rules and common customs like everyone else in Galilee. Embracing the accepted way of everyday life, he will have conformed spontaneously to a number of biblical precepts. The Gospels show him also complying with the laws regulating religious activity proper, participating in synagogue worship on the sabbath, visiting the Temple of Jerusalem as a pilgrim, and celebrating the Passover. Some scholars deduce from the references to the *kraspedon*, the hem or tassel of Jesus's robe (Mark 6:56), that he must have been a strict observer of the Torah (Num. 15:38–39), but he may simply have dressed like his fellow Galileans. If his own tassels, or *ziziyoth*, had been unusually long, he would hardly have criticized others for displaying them too ostentatiously (Matt. 23:5).

More important, though still not particularly meaningful, is the selection Jesus makes of certain biblical commandments as summarizing the individual laws of the Old Testament. There was a general tendency among Jews in the early postbiblical centuries to discover a small number of all-inclusive precepts. The fullest illustration of this trend comes from Rabbi Simlai, a third century C.E. sage, who explains that all 613 positive and negative commandments proclaimed by Moses were, according to David (Ps. 15), contained in eleven; acording to Isaiah (33:15), in six; according to Micah (6:8), in three (to do justice, love mercy, and walk humbly with God); according to Isaiah again (56:1), in two (to observe justice and do righteousness); and according to Amos (5:4), in one alone, "Seek me and live." Both Jesus and Philo, his Alexandrian Jewish contemporary, maintained that the Decalogue symbolizes all the "special laws" of the Torah. When asked what must be done to inherit eternal life, Jesus merely recites from the Ten Commandments: "Do not kill! Do not commit adultery! Do not steal!" (Mark 10:19) And when invited to reduce the many to one, he chooses the first or great commandment in its twofold aspect of love: "You shall love the Lord your God . . . and your neighbour as yourself!" (Mark 12:29–31). At the same time, when there is question of a comprehensive counsel of behavior, his one-article code—accredited also, though in a different form, to the great Hillel (Babylonian Talmud–Shabbath 31a), who may have still been alive when Jesus was born—explicitly prescribes the single duty, "Whatever you wish that men should do to you, do so to them!" Matthew adds, "For this is the Law and the Prophets" (Matt. 7:12; Luke 6:31).

But has it not been asserted through the centuries that Jesus frees man from "the curse of the Law" (Gal. 3:13), that he substitutes for the Law a new dispensation of grace? Indeed it has, but in echo only, as we shall see, of the voice of the Diaspora Hellenist, Paul of Tarsus, not that of the Galilean. He, according to reliable Gospel evidence, excuses no neglect of the Law as such. Reminiscent of many a rabbinic dictum, his words as reported by Luke, himself a Greek addressing Gentiles, leaves no room for doubt concerning Jesus's own attitude: "It is easier for heaven and earth to pass away than for one tittle of the Law to fall" (Luke 16:17; Matt. 5:18).

The controversial sayings attributed to him in the Gospels are to be seen against this faithfulness to the Torah. Some of the arguments have to do with the interpretation of customs, such as hand washing before meals, but most are associated with the sabbath and its observance. Jewish legal teaching (*halakah*) was still in a fluid state in his time; the great effort of unification and definition resulting in so-called orthodoxy was not made until after A.D. 70. He is often charged by New Testament exegetes, mostly on the basis of a gloss appended by Mark to a paradoxical question posed by Jesus, with having rejected the dietary laws. "Do you not see that nothing that goes from outside into a man can defile him," Mark gives Jesus to inquire, adding as his own observation, "Thus he declared all foods clean" (Mark 7:18–19). But on reflection, are we not bound to conclude a priori that, in a Palestinian environment, the abolition of all distinction between pure and impure food is almost inconceivable. Besides, what about the historically dependable claim in the Acts of the Apostles that Jesus's immediate followers found the very idea of touching forbidden food horrible and scandalous (Acts 10:13–16). For them, as appears from Paul's angry criticism, table companionship with Gentile Christians was intolerable and shameful (Gal.

2:11–14). The Marcan comment will have catered for non-Jewish members of the church unprepared to be bothered with such rules.

Furthermore, the Gospels themselves often involve Jesus in polemics relating to observance of the sabbath. The main point to remember here is that in Judaism the saving of life takes precedence over sabbath laws (Mekhilta on Ex. 31:12). Indeed, during the bloody Hadrianic persecution, a hundred years after the time of Jesus, the rabbis accorded it primacy over all laws with the exception of idolatry, incest, and murder. The text from Leviticus (18:5), "You shall keep my statutes . . . by which a man shall live," was interpreted to mean that observance of the torah should not lead to death (Bab. Talm.–Shab. 74a). In the case of Jesus's sabbath debates, where the subject at issue is almost always healing, the principle emerging from them appears to be that every cure, great or small, is a saving of life. The restoration to health of a man with a paralyzed hand is as serious as deliverance from death, and as cogent a justification for infringing the sabbath (Matt. 12:9–14; Luke 14:1–6): that is, should justification be necessary when the cure is performed by word of mouth alone, without any accompanying "work" such as carrying or administering medicines.

Jesus not only submits personally to the legal obligations incumbent on a Jew; he more than once expressly urges obedience to the purely ritual and cultic precepts in sayings all the more historically credible in that they are peripheral to the Gospel narrative, and actually run counter to the essential antinomianism of Gentile Christianity. Having cured several lepers, he orders them to report to the priests and to perform the ceremony prescribed by Moses (Mark 1:44; Luke 17:14). He approves of sending gifts to the Temple (Matt. 5:23), and of the tithing laws which were not very popular with the Galilean countryfolk (Matt. 23:23; Luke 11:42). He is even depicted, though I doubt the authenticity of the actual statement, as giving support to the theory, if not the practice, of Pharisee legal teaching (Matt 23:2–3).

Where the Law is concerned, the real distinction of Jesus's piety lies in his extraordinary emphasis on the real inner religious significance of the commandments. He was naturally not alone among Jewish teachers to insist on inwardness and sincerity. Philo did the same. So did many of the rabbis, and occasionally the Qumran sectaries. But I believe that interiority, purity of intention, played a greater part in Jesus's thought possibly because of the combination of his stress on eschatological finality with his natural bias toward the individual and the personal rather than the collective. He tends in any case to lay a heavy, and sometimes almost exaggerated, accent on the primary causes and ultimate aim of the religious or irreligious act. Murder has its roots in anger; adultery, in the lustful gaze. His followers must therefore avoid the lesser faults as scrupulously as they would shun the greater. Similarly, he clearly regards the ritual impurity contracted through transgressing the dietary laws as insignificant compared with the uncleanness of "fornication, theft, murder, adultery, . . . envy, slander, pride, foolishness" (Mark 7:14–23; Matt. 15:10–20). His teaching is that excretion defiles more than ingestion, and that nothing defiles more foully than the excretion of the wicked heart with its evil thoughts.

Exactly the same principle underlies Jesus's attitude to almsgiving, prayer, and fasting. They stand or fall as religious acts in proportion to the integrity with which they are performed. Charitable gifts must be made in secret, without witnesses. Prayer is to be offered in private, not aloud in the streets or in the synagogue. Fasting is to be undertaken with a smiling face, before God alone (Matt 6:1–8, 16–18).

Jesus's religious deed was done, in other words, in accordance with Jewish religious Law and laws. But it was invested with an added dimension of effectiveness and power through his genial perception of the Law's innermost significance, of what it was originally intended to be: namely, a vehicle for authentic lived relation with God the Father, God the King.

Before examining the concrete manifestations of this God/man— Father/Son relation as it is attested in the synoptic Gospels, brief mention must be made of a few framentary statements somewhat theoretical in their stand vis-à-vis God. They may all ultimately derive from the primitive church, but more probably they may be in part representative of Jesus's thought, and in part ecclesiastical formulations.

The first is the celebrated thanksgiving recorded in Matthew (11:27) and Luke (10:22). "All things have been delivered to me by my Father; and no one knows who the son is except the Father, or who the Father is, except the son, and anyone to whom the son chooses to reveal him." Whether the idea of revelation contained in this text reflects a Hellenistic milieu or an Aramaic wisdom school, or whether it is akin to the sort of knowledge-speculation found in the Dead Sea Scrolls, is secondary and almost immaterial compared with the fundamental concept, expressed by the evangelists with great perspicuity, of an ideal reciprocity between Father and Son. This reciprocity is not equality. It is a remarkable fact that the Father's superiority remains impregnable even in face of the church's editorial intervention. The *panta,* all things, revealed to Jesus by the Father do not include that most crucial of all knowledge, knowledge of the end time. Of that day and hour it is said, "no one knows, not even the angels in heaven, nor the son, but only the Father" (Mark 12:32; Matt. 24:36). This passage, despite the dubious authenticity of the eschatological discourse into which it is inserted, is more likely to be genuine in that it conflicts with later church doctrine endowing Christ with perfect wisdom. Similarly, when the two ambitious apostles, James and John, wish to secure for themselves the best places in the kingdom, they are told, "To sit at my right hand and at my left is not mine to grant, but it is for those for whom it has been prepared by my Father" (Matt. 20:23; Mark 10:40).

These apparently dogmatic statements about God must not mislead us. It was not Jesus's habit to theorize about the Divine. His preoccupation was with enacting to perfection, in his own person, the role of son, of child, of the Father in heaven, and with teaching his followers to live likewise. "Ask," he instructs them, "and it shall be given you; seek and you shall find; knock and it shall be opened to you." Would any of them, entreated by their children for bread, give them a stone? Or a snake instead of some fish? "If you, then, who are evil, know how to give good gifts to your children, how much more will your Father who is in heaven give good things to those who ask him?" (Matt. 7:7–11; Luke 11:9–13). And even this occasional asking is not enough; God's children have to implore their Father daily for the day's needs (Matt. 6:11; Luke 11:3). They must *pester* him, like little children, until he grants them their desire. Or, adopting another metaphor, they must imitate the man who, to feed an unexpected visitor, woke his friend in the middle of the night and importuned him until he got out of bed and lent him three loaves of bread (Luke 11:5–8).

The total simplicity and confidence required of the child of God as Jesus represents him is the biblical *emunah* (faith/trust), the virtue which, according to Martin Buber (1951, 28–29), Jesus and the prophets possessed in common. It may also point to an inheritance from ancient Hasidism, where the same spirit prevailed. The first century B.C.E. charismatic, Honi (or Onias the Righteous, as Flavius Josephus names him), is famous for his petulant threat that he would not step outside the circle which he had drawn around himself until God showed mercy to his children and ended the long season of drought. Honi's behavior is said to have provoked Simeon ben Shetah, the leading Pharisee of that time, to comment resentfully: "If you were not Honi, I would excommunicate you [because of your disrespect]. But what can I do with you, since even though you importune God, he does what you want" (Mishnah–Taanith 3 : 8). The rabbis were sticklers for correct behavior and disapproved of temerity such as Honi's, but they were compelled to confess that it sometimes worked. "*Huzpa*," impertinence, "has its usefulness even towards heaven," reads the Babylonian Talmud (Sanhedrin 105a). It is *emunah*, also, that characterizes Jesus's recommendation that the child of God should lay aside material and temporal anxieties and commit itself wholly to the care of the Father in heaven. "Do not be anxious about your life," the Galilean urges,

> what you shall eat . . . , nor about your body, what you shall put on. . . . Look at the birds of the air: they neither sow nor reap nor gather into barns, and yet your heavenly Father feeds them. Are you not of more value than they? . . . And why are you anxious about your clothing? Consider the lilies of the field, how they grow; they neither toil, nor spin; yet I tell you, even Solomon in all his glory was not arrayed like one of these. . . . Therefore do not be anxious, saying, "What shall we eat?" or "What shall we drink?" or "What shall we wear?" . . . Your heavenly Father knows that you need them all. (Matt. 6 : 25–34; Luke 12 : 22–31)

And Jesus asks further: "Are not two small birds sold for an *assarion* and not one of them shall fall to the ground without your Father's will. . . . Fear not therefore; you are of more value than many sparrows" (Matt. 10 : 29–31; Luke 12 : 6–7).

As might be expected, the counterpart of the sort of unconditional surrender to Divine Providence demanded of his followers by Jesus is a condemnation and rejection of man-made plans and projects, long-term and short. The futility of trying to count on and provide for the future is illustrated in the parable of the rich landowner who, with a good harvest in view, thinks of pulling down his barns and replacing them with larger ones, with the idea of ensuring his future prosperity with much food, drink, and merriment for years to come. But Jesus exclaims: "Fool! Tonight your soul is required of you; and the things you have prepared, whose will they be?" (Luke 12:16–20). Even when the immediate future is concerned, his thought extends no further than to the requirements of the day, to the "*daily* bread" (Matt. 6:11; Luke 11:13). Directly and explicitly, his counsel in the Sermon on the Mount is: "Do not be anxious about tomorrow, for tomorrow will be anxious for itself. Let the day's own trouble be sufficient for the day" (Matt. 6:34). Jesus was a man for whom the present, the here and now, was of unique and inifinite importance.

It may be this exclusive concentration on the religious task immediately facing him, inspired by an "enthusiasm [born] of eschatological presence," to borrow again from Martin Buber (1951, 76), that accounts for Jesus's total lack of interest in the economic and political realities of his age. For he was not a social reformer, or a nationalistic revolutionary, notwithstanding recent claims to the contrary. Nor did the urgency of his religious vision allow any place for founding, organizing, and endowing with permanency an ecclesiastical body of any sort. It was rather the extinction of the parousia hope, cultivated in self-contained primitive Christian communities, that conferred durability on a fabric intended by the apostles and the first disciples to last no longer than a brief span.

Foresight, farsightedness make better sense within the context of expectation of a Second Coming, or where the spirit of eschatological presence has died away, than in the thought of Jesus. The parable of the wise virgins—supposedly wise, but to my mind cunning and selfish—reflects an insistence on the part of the church to be constantly ready; it contributes nothing to any active participation in the work of the kingdom of God. The young women, foreseeing that the bridegroom may be late, bring with them a good supply of oil for their lamps. But they refuse to share it with their "foolish" friends. They send them off to find dealers at midnight. And by the time they return, the gate is closed. When they ask to be let in, no one admits them (Matt. 25:1–13). Did Matthew or his later editor not realize that this parable is a travesty of the teachings on generosity and confident prayer contained in the same Gospel?

By comparison with the kingdom and its coming, and the affairs of the heavenly Father, everything temporal becomes of secondary importance. All that matters is action, *now*. There can be no procrastination, no dawdling; "The Kingdom of God is at hand" (Mark 1:15). The disciple must follow the teacher's call, at once. He must not ask for permission to go home and say goodbye to his family, for no man "who puts his hand to the plough and looks back is fit for the Kingdom of God" (Luke 9:61–62). He must not return and bury his father (Matt. 8: 21–22; Luke 9:59–60). "Leave the dead to bury their dead" is the paradoxical command. Also, solemn family ties must take second place to the bond uniting those who do God's will. As Jesus remarks of his waiting relations, "Who are my mother and my brothers? . . . Whoever does the will of God is my brother, and sister and mother" (Mark 3:33–34).

Two important parables adumbrate the single-minded devotion to the cause of the Father which Jesus promoted and the prompt and decisive action which he required of those who seek to enter the kingdom. In the first, where it is compared to a treasure discovered in a field, the finder covers it over, and "then in joy he goes and sells all he has and buys that field" (Matt. 13:44). In the second, where it is compared to a pearl of great value, a merchant of pearls, noticing it, "went and sold all that he had and bought it" (Matt. 13:45–46). In both parables, the lesson is identical. On encountering the truth, a choice has to be made, a decision, and it must be acted on immediately, wholeheartedly. A price must be paid for it, one which will amount to all that one has.

Now that we know something of the workings of Jesus's mind, of the pressures to which he subjected it, and of the values on which he laid the greatest stress, one fundamental question forms itself—namely, what in the last resort was the principle that he adopted, and himself embodied, in his endeavors to live to perfection as a son of God? The reply must be that it was the principle, well attested in Judaism, biblical and post-biblical, of the *imitatio dei,* the imitation of God. "You shall be holy, for I the Lord, your God, am holy" (Lev. 19:2).

Rabbinic thought is rich in interpretation of this theme that the lover and worshipper of God models himself on him. Confronted with the verse (Exod. 15:2), "This is my God, and I will praise him" (*we'an-*

*wehu*), the second century sage, Abba Shaul, reads instead, "This is my God, I and He" (*'ani wa-hu*), expounding the last clause as, "O be like Him! As He is merciful and gracious, you also must be merciful and gracious" (Mekhilta on Exod. 15:2). Similarly, but entering into details, an anonymous exegete comments apropos of the words of Deuteronomy (10:12), "that you may walk in His ways." He points out, "These are the ways of God, 'The Lord, a God merciful and gracious . . .' [Exod. 34:6]. 'All who are called by the name of the Lord shall be delivered' [Joel 3:5; Engl. 2:32]. How can a man be called by the name of God? As God is called merciful, you too must be merciful. The Holy One blessed be He is called gracious, so you too must be gracious . . . and give presents freely. God is called righteous . . . so you too must be righteous" (*Siphre on Deuteronomy*, par. 49). But one of the most succinct renderings of this doctrine of the *imitatio dei* is given in an Aramaic paraphrase of Leviticus. "My people, children of Israel, as your Father is merciful in heaven, so you must be merciful on earth" (Targum Ps.—Jonathan on Leviticus 22:28).

Jesus proclaims the same basic teachings—"Be merciful as your Father is merciful" (Luke 6:36), and "Be perfect as your heavenly Father is perfect" (Matt. 5:48)—but injects them with his own extra dimension of integrity and inwardness. Perfect filial behavior in imitation of the Father must show itself not simply in mercy and love toward others, but in a mercy and love that expects no return. "You received without paying, give without payment," he says (Matt. 10:8). On another occasion, he speaks more forcefully still. "When you give a dinner or a banquet, do not invite your friends or your brothers or your kinsmen or rich neighbours, lest they also invite you in return, and you be repaid. But when you give a feast, invite the poor, the maimed, the lame and the blind, and you will be blessed, because they cannot repay you" (Luke 14:12–14).

This is his usual custom: to opt for a maximum of exaggeration in order to underline what he is attempting to convey. No teaching exemplifies this better than the command to his disciples to love their enemies. The saying has been the source of much misunderstanding and misinterpretation, for there is no denying that to love persons motivated by hatred of oneself, or who subject one to abuse and persecution, must seem unnatural and humanly impossible. But Jesus's words are no more to be taken literally than in that other text requiring the would-be follower to hate his father, mother, wife, children, brothers, and sisters (Luke 14:26); or than his instruction to his disciples, "To him who strikes you on the cheek, offer the other also" (Luke 6:29; Matt. 5:39). The independent Passion narrative of the Fourth Gospel in no way bears out this last piece of advice. When an overzealous policeman slaps his face, Jesus does not turn the other cheek but protests with dignity, "If I have spoken wrongly, bear witness to the wrong, but if I have spoken rightly, why do you strike me?" (John 18:24). The commandment to love one's enemies is an overstatement intended to impress on his hearers that the perfect manifestation of love is to offer it quite freely, gratis. "Love your enemies, do good to those who hate you, bless those who curse you, pray for those who abuse you. . . . If you love those who love you, what credit is that to you . . . ? And if you do good to those who do good to you, what credit is that to you . . . ? And if you lend to those from whom you expect to receive, what credit is that to you . . . ? But love your enemies, and do good and lend, expecting nothing in return . . . and you will be sons of the Most High" (Luke 6:27–35)—"sons of your Father who is in heaven" (Matt. 5:45).

Jesus's righteousness, the piety peculiar to Jesus the religious man, is marked by a tendency to give more than is asked for, to probe deeper than expected, to risk more than is safe. The neighbors he is to love as himself often turn out to be the outcasts of society whose company he does not merely accept but positively seeks (Luke 15:1). Unlike the pious of his day and of later times, he enters their houses and eats with them (Mark 2:15). He even (scandal of scandals) allows a prostitute to anoint him (Luke 7:37–38). He treats them as friends; hence the sarcastic nickname conferred on him by his critics—"friend of tax-collectors and sinners" (Matt. 11:19; Luke 7:34). But his behavior should cause no surprise. He is simply imitating in his personal conduct what he understands will be the conduct of the Father toward those of his children who turn from a state of absence from God to a relation with him. "There will be," he maintains, "more joy in heaven over one sinner who repents than over ninety-nine just" (Luke 15:7).

Turning now to Christian religion and religiousness as distinct from the religiousness and religion of Jesus, I am aware that for the vast majority of Christians, and many Jews, the very statement that Jesus and

Christianity are to be differentiated one from the other will come as a shock. Present-day Christians are in the main wholly innocent of the gulf dividing their aims and beliefs from his.

I will now reduce to its essentials my exposition of the Gospel of Jesus the Jew and to set alongside it a basic sketch of Christianity almost exclusively with the help of the doctrine on which it rests: the teaching of Paul, the source from which arose the institutional, ecclesiastical religious body, professing a creed, known as Christianity.

Before developing my argument, I must clarify one point. I have been accused of distorting Paul's views. He was a complex personality, and I would not presume to portray his many-colored and often changing ideas in a page or two. What I propose to do is to describe summarily the impact of Paul on the early Church and place in relief the imprint of his message on real Christianity.

The first marked dissimilarity lies in the Jewishness of Jesus, his environment, his way of life, his purpose. It is a Jewishness that sometimes amounts to downright chauvinism, as is apparent from the unflattering epithets which the blunt Galilean lets fly against non-Jews. "Dogs," he observes of them, which are not to eat of the bread belonging to the children (Mark 7:27; Matt. 15:26) or partake of the "holy things" (Matt. 7:6), "swine" on which his apostles are not to waste the pearls of their teaching. Do not trouble yourselves with them, he explicitly enjoins on another occasion. "Go nowhere among the Gentiles . . . but rather to the lost sheep of the house of Israel" (Matt. 10:5–6; 15:24).

But however did the evangelists manage to record such sayings and at the same time attribute to Jesus the view that the Gentiles were soon to displace "the sons of the Kingdom," the Jews, as the elect of God (Matt. 8:11–12; Luke 13:28–29)? I would suggest that once Paul was acknowledged "apostle to the Gentiles" (Acts 9:15; Rom. 11:13) and a specifically Gentile mission sanctioned by the church leadership came into being (Acts 15), the original bias of Jesus's ministry underwent a radical transformation. Gentiles in substantial numbers joined the ranks of the church which, following the model of proselytism in Judaism (flourishing in those days), did its best to comply with the needs of the new situation and to adjust itself to altered circumstances. Moreover, Paul's pronouncement that the Christian communities now formed the "Israel of God" (Gal. 6:16) would have neutralized the sting of the insults so oddly preserved in the Gospel text. The Gentile followers of Jesus, advised to consider themselves henceforth as "neither Jew nor Greek" (Gal. 3:28), would have been persuaded that it was not they who were the target of their Lord's contempt.

It is possible, incidentally, to argue that an element of universalism is not absent from the inner logic of Jesus's teaching. It can be detected for example in the commandment to love one's enemies, which implies that they are fellow creatures under the one God to whom charity must be shown, in imitation of the Father of all who cares for all.

Another enormous change arising from the transplantation of the Christian movement into Gentile soil, one that affected its very nature, was that, despite Jesus's injunctions to the contrary, the Torah, the source of his inspiration and the discipline ruling his religious life, was declared by the church to be not merely optional but revoked, abolished, superseded. The Law which he had understood with such simplicity and profundity, and carried out with such integrity, in accordance with what he saw to be its inmost truth, was judged by Paul to be in practice an instrument of sin and death. "Christ," he declared, "is the end of the Law" (Rom. 10:4).

Nevertheless, if Jesus and Christianity seem to stand worlds apart on this issue, neither Paul nor the later church pushed antinomianism so far as to apply to the ethical sphere. There is no denying that the heart of Jesus's message, with its stress on interiority and supererogation, was heard by the early church, and has indeed remained intrinsic to the ideal of individual Christian piety: an ideal on which organized public ecclesiastical piety in its various manifestations has acted as a brake and corrective.

With that, we arrive at one more radical distinction. The lifeblood of Jesus's mission was eschatological urgency. He believed and taught that the kingdom of God was actually, at that time, in the process of coming into being, and that it would be fully established in the immediate future. As we know, this did not happen. The eagerness and excitement then transferred itself to hope in a second advent of Christ. But once again, it did not happen. He did not come. The resulting emptiness had therefore to be made good and a corporate body took shape as a quasi-permanent substitute kingdom which would serve as a repository of religion until the glorious return of Christ the King at the end of days.

And what happened to Jesus's imitation of God within the framework of this institutional church? Primitive Christianity was certainly conscious of it and promulgated it as a rule to be followed. "Be imitators of God as beloved children," Paul writes to the Ephesians (5 : 1). And yet it was this same Paul who was responsible for giving a twist to the *imitatio dei*, which opened up a great divide between Judaism and Christianity. "Be imitators of me as I am of Christ" (1 Cor. 11 : 1). With these words, Paul, deviating from the Jewish imitation of God, introduces intermediaries between the imitator and his ultimate divine model. First of all, imitate me, who am an imitator of Jesus, who imitated God. Thus originated the trend, still conspicuous in the more ancient forms of Christianity, to multiply mediators and intercessors between the faithful and God: Jesus, Paul, Mary the mother of Jesus, the martyrs, the saints.

This question of intermediaries brings us in effect to the crux of the problem: that the example of Jesus's *hasiduth*, of his theocentric devoutness, has been overlaid by the ramifications of Paul's Christocentric spirituality. Paul's opinion of human nature was deeply pessimistic. In his view, man is sinful, incapable of obeying God, potentially damned and lost without the saving grace of Christ's atoning death. Christ's sacrificial blood is essential to the cleansing of his sins. Except for the redemption obtained by Christ's passion and resurrection, he can never draw close to God. God "sent forth his son . . . born under the law, to redeem those who were under the law, so that we might receive adoption as sons" (Gal. 4 : 4−5). With increasing vehemence, the religiosity of primitive Christianity became trained on the mediator in place of God. Prayers continued to be addressed to the Father, but more and more frequently to "the Father of our Lord Jesus Christ" (Rom. 15 : 6; 2 Cor. 1 : 3, 11−31). Little by little, the Christ of Pauline theology and his Gentile church took over from the holy man of Galilee. Subject to God but already enthroned at his side, he then (no doubt in response to the needs and hopes of non-Jewish Christianity) imperceptibly grew to be the "image of God," the "effulgence of God's glory and the stamp of his nature," and finally, the equal of God (1 Cor. 15 : 28; 2 Cor. 4 : 4; Heb. 1 : 3). Writes Ignatius bishop of Antioch to Polycarp bishop of Smyrna, in the first decade of the second century, "I bid you farewell always in our God Jesus Christ" (Epistle to Polycarp 8).

And the real Jesus? For there was a real Jesus, without any doubt.

Over the space of months, or perhaps even of two or three years, a Jesus of flesh and blood was seen and heard around the countryside of Galilee and in Jerusalem, an uncompromising, single-minded lover of God and his fellow beings, convinced that by means of his example and teaching he could infect others with his own passionate sense of relation with the Father in heaven. And he did. The magnetism of this real Jesus was such that not even the shame and humiliation of the cross, and not even the collapse of his ministry, could extinguish the faith of the men and women of his company. But it is a long time now since he was thought of. Very many ages have passed since the simple Jewish person of the Gospels stepped back and gave way to the rich and majestic figure of the church's Christ.

Yet it occurs to the historian that Jews, Christians, and the world may not have heard the last of the holy Galilean. In this so-called post-Christian era, when Christ as a divine form seems to ever-increasing numbers not to correspond either to the age's notion of reality or to the exigencies of the contemporary human predicament, is it possible that Jesus the healer, teacher, and helper may be invited to emerge from the shadows of his long exile? And not by Christians alone? If, above all, his lesson on reciprocal, loving, and direct relation with the Father in heaven is remembered and found valid, may not the sons of God on earth stand a better chance of ensuring that the ideal of human brotherhood becomes something more than a pipe dream?


## Literature Cited

Buber, Martin. *Two Types of Faith*. Harper Torchbooks, New York, 1951.
Manson, Thomas Walter. *The Teaching of Jesus*. Cambridge University Press, Cambridge, 1935.